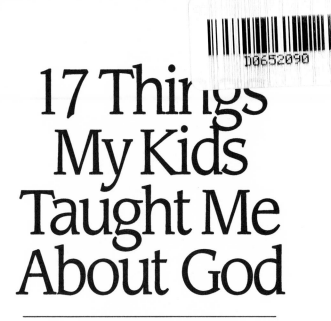

17 Things My Kids Taught Me About God

PARABLES
OF SPIRITUAL
SIGHT

J. MACK STILES

InterVarsity Press
Downers Grove, Illinois

InterVarsity Press
P.O. Box 1400, Downers Grove, IL 60515
World Wide Web: www.ivpress.com
E-mail: mail@ivpress.com

InterVarsity Press® is the book-publishing division of InterVarsity Christian
Fellowship/USA®, a student movement active on campus at hundreds of universities,
colleges and schools of nursing in the United States of America, and a member movement of the International Fellowship of Evangelical Students. For information about
local and regional activities, write Public Relations Dept., InterVarsity Christian
Fellowship/USA, 6400 Schroeder Rd., P.O. Box 7895, Madison, WI 53707-7895.

Cover photograph: Michael Goss

ISBN 0-8308-1927-4

Printed in the United States of America ♾

Library of Congress Cataloging-in-Publication Data
Stiles, J. Mack, 1956-
    17 things my kids taught me about God : parables of spiritual sight / J. Mack
Stiles.
        p.   cm.
    ISBN 0-8308-1927-4 (pbk. : alk. paper)
    1. Christian life.   2. Children—Religious life.   3. Stiles, J. Mack, 1956—Family rela-
tionships.   4. Family—Religious life.
I. Title.   II. Title: Seventeen things my kids taught me about God.
BV4501.2.S764   1998
242—DC21   98-18497
                                                                            CIP

15	14	13	12	11	10	9	8	7	6	5	4	3	2	1
08	07	06	05	04	03	02	01	00	99	98				

To Leeann, whose love has carried me

Acknowledgments

There are so many who helped this book come to be.

I'm grateful for Jeannie Musick, Mark Dever (along with Connie, Annie and Nathan) and Tony Warner for helping me think through this book in its earliest form.

Special thanks to First Alliance Church of Lexington, which allowed me to present a number of chapters in this book from the pulpit.

Thanks to teachers and staff at Maxwell Elementary Spanish Immersion School.

Jim and Beth Reed graciously allowed us the use of their "Bird House" at Scotland Cay, where I began and ended this book.

Thanks to Andy Le Peau, who provided the wisdom and leadership every writer hopes for from an editor.

I want to thank the college students across the United States and Canada involved in InterVarsity Christian Fellowship who have welcomed me to their fellowships, camps and conferences.

And special thanks to IVCF staff in the Southeast, who have loved and supported me.

Introduction

You may think it strange for me to write a book about grow-ing into spiritual maturity using stories of my kids. It's not the literary equivalent of home movies, I promise. It's that I find watching my children helps me develop spiritual sight. This happens in two very different ways.

Sometimes I find myself in an almost Godlike position with my children. I know I'm not God, but at times my view of their life from an adult's eyes gives me an overarching perspective that helps me understand what God sees when he's dealing with me.

At other times it's the opposite. Children's perspectives on the world can be the Godlike one: uncorrupted spirits reflect-ing a faith commended by Jesus. They see the spiritual world in clear focus.

I have three sons, Tristan, David and Isaac, who at the time of this writing are ten, eight and six. I'm grateful for their love for their dad. I'm grateful too for their excitement about this book. They also want it to be helpful.

These stories are ours, and they are true stories. But in one story or two I've moved the name of one brother to the other. In some stories that are not about our family I've changed names to protect privacy.

The goal of this book is to help you develop spiritual sight. Whether I see from the perspective of God or see God through my sons' perspective, I find that both help me to see Jesus. I hope it will be so for you too.

Sight

*One thing
I do know.
I was blind
but now I see!*

JOHN 9:25

1

Angels
in the
Bedroom

W*hen you* were a kid, did you ever wake up in the dark of night with the vague feeling that something had crept beneath your bed while you slept? You didn't dare look, but you heard its slow breathing. It lurked there waiting for the right moment to grab your ankle and drag you under if you tried to get out of bed. So you slept completely covered under the blankets—muggy, but safe.

The basement held terror for me. I came to an agreement with the goblins that lived down there: I played in the light, they played in the dark. The traumatic moment would come when our times overlapped. My parents required me to turn off the lights when I finished playing in the basement, but there was only one switch, and it was a couple of feet from the stairs, so I was forced to scramble to the top in the dark. I'm convinced that the creepy dash from switch to landing fostered my love of running.

Today my son David reports that monsters have grown in our basement as well, though he says with authority, "They never come upstairs." Our light switch is sensibly placed at both the top and the bottom of our basement stairs—the builder must have been scared of the dark too.

Nightmares and Guardian Angels

Childhood fears are innumerable, but I don't think there is anything more scary than the scary dream.

My firstborn son, Tristan, five years old at the time, studied the passing scenery from his perch in his booster seat while we ran errands on an autumn afternoon. When we got to the shopping complex, Tristan piped up, "Dad, I had a scary dream last night."

"I'm sorry, Tristan." I smiled to myself, thinking about scary dreams I had when I was little. "Sometimes dreams are really scary, aren't they?" I said.

"Yeah," he said.

"But you know, Tristan, you gotta remember it's just a dream."

"Yeah," he repeated.

After some thought I asked, "Why didn't you call for me or Mom?" This is standard operating procedure for scary dreams in our house (bringing with it the most dangerous part of scary dreams: my sleepy, bumbling journey to their room in the dark while avoiding small metal cars strewn on the floor).

"Well," he said, "when I woke up I was too scared to even talk."

I remember that feeling. "Poor kid," I said.

"But it didn't matter," he continued. "I prayed, and God sent an angel to take care of me."

I smiled again. "That's great, Tristan. It's a good thing Mom prays every night for God's angels to surround you, isn't it?"

"Yeah."

I didn't mean to patronize him, sitting there in his booster seat pondering angels. I pulled into the line at the dry cleaner to pick up the laundry.

"What are angels, Dad?"

"Well, angels are God's messengers and servants, and God uses them to protect his people." I said. "Jesus said the angels of children look in the face of God" (Matthew 18:10).

Tristan nodded knowingly.

We fell silent as I hung my clean shirts in the back and began my hunt for a parking place in the sea of glinting cars spread out in front of the grocery store.

"He had a shiny face."

"Who did, Tristan?"

"The angel last night. His face was like looking at a light bulb, only different."

I cocked my head and gave him a sidelong glance. This didn't sound like a dream.

"Hey, Dad, you know how everyone says angels have wings?"

"Uh-huh," I said as I switched off the car and sat back in the seat so we could talk about this a bit more.

"They don't have wings."

"They don't?"

"Well, the angel last night didn't."

"He didn't?" I said slowly. *Maybe Tristan really saw something last night,* I thought to myself. "Tristan, um, did you talk to him?" Now I was the one asking questions, and Tristan was matter-of-fact.

"Oh no," he said. "I was too scared to do that."

"Scared because you were dreaming?"

"No, I wasn't scared of the dream after the angel came. He told me not to be afraid, and I saw his face bending down over me. I was too scared of the angel. That's why I didn't talk to the angel."

"Why were you scared of the angel, Tristan?"

"He was big."

"Big?"

"Yeah . . . I mean he could fit in the room and everything, but he had to sit down."

My smile changed to a look of astonishment. Tristan watched people push their shopping carts by our car.

He continued. "It was a different kind of scared, 'cause I knew he was there to take care of me."

"How did you know that?"

"Daddy," he said emphatically, "I prayed!"

"Oh yeah, that's right," I said. This felt uncomfortably similar to the story of Elisha's servant. Elisha's servant was frightened too. And, like Tristan, he had his eyes opened to spiritual reality.

Chariots of God

In the days of the kings of Israel, Elisha's prophetic warnings protected Israel from the attacks of their enemies. But when this fact became known, the enemies surrounded Elisha's hometown of Dothan to take him captive. Elisha's servant spied the enemy's horses and chariots surrounding the city and ran to Elisha in panic.

"Oh, my lord, what shall we do?" the servant asked. "Don't be afraid," the prophet answered. . . . And Elisha prayed, "O LORD, open his eyes so he may see." Then the LORD opened the servant's eyes, and he looked and saw the hills full of horses and chariots of fire all around Elisha. (2 Kings 6:15-17)

Elisha's prayer for his servant was for him to see spiritual reality. To see, as Elisha said, that "those who are with us are more than those who are with them." Or, as John said years later, "The one who is in you is greater than the one who is in the world" (1 John 4:4). God's aim for us is not that we see angels but that we see the big picture. Any parent who deals with his or her children's fears understands this.

Notice that this is more a result of prayer (for Elisha and Tristan) than it is of seeing angels. I suppose God could have made us connect with the spiritual world by using the direction of the stars in a daily horoscope. At his command we might have used Ouija boards or crystal balls or palm reading or mediums who take our money with 1-900 phone numbers, for that matter, but he didn't—in fact he hates that stuff because they lie. Our connection with the spiritual world—prayer—should be personal, simple and childlike.

Prayer and the Big Picture

The best part of prayer is not getting our shopping list checked off by God, but having our sight aligned with his. Prayer helps us focus on the big spiritual picture; prayerlessness says that everything we see is all there is.

Jesus had the same desire for his disciples as Elisha did for his servant. From Jerusalem to Jezreel Jesus wanted his disciples to see the big spiritual picture. There is a striking parallel between Elisha's prayer in Dothan and Jesus' prayer in the garden of Gethsemane. Both were surrounded by armed men waiting to arrest them. Both had fearful servants who did not understand spiritual reality. Both saw clearly who was on their side. Jesus told his disciples: "Do you think I cannot call on my Father, and he will at once put at my disposal more than twelve legions of angels?" (Matthew 26:53).

There was one major difference, however. Jesus could have called on angels, but he didn't. He saw an even greater spiritual reality—the need to give his life as an atoning sacrifice. For that I'm eternally grateful.

But just for the record, twelve legions of angels is between fifty-four thousand and seventy-two thousand angels. And Tristan tells me they're big . . . "really big."

"Daddy?"

"Yes, Tristan."

"What do the angels *you* see look like?"

"Well, Tristan, I don't remember, but I know this: next time something scary happens, I want to be with you. You've got a big angel."

2

Armageddon
in the
Back Yard

We lifted our heads from singing our evening blessing—the Johnny Appleseed prayer. Putting the sights of the beautiful autumn evening behind us, we began devouring the meal. Serving plates soon lay empty on the table. Table banter mixed with the clinks of forks and our preschool plaster-of-Paris wind chime. Isaac directed my preparation of his baked potato, Tristan told us of his Lego project under construction in his room, and Leeann told me the latest PTA news.

Not too long into the meal I noticed David staring across our back yard to the rolling Kentucky pasture behind our house. There was nothing unusual about this; observant boys notice lots of exciting things happening there—the neighborhood cat on the prowl, a groundhog out for a stroll, a hawk fluttering over its prey. What was unusual was David's look of terror.

David tends to notice everything going on around him. This is a blessing and a curse. When David's coach played him at the goalie position his first season of soccer, he did really well until a passing train captured his attention, allowing the other team to score two goals before the train moved on. (David told us trains were more interesting than the game, and we were forced to agree.) But there are also times when his laserlike focus gives him a mystical view of things.

As the sun's descent met the far hill, a fiery glint burst out across the field, making both the hilltop and the field appear aflame. But far from appreciating this gorgeous display of nature, David opened his eyes wide with fear and burst into tears.

We all began asking David what the matter was, but he wept so hard it was difficult to understand what he was saying (especially with his mouth full of chicken). His eyes never left the sunset.

"Oh, I'm scared, I'm scared, I'm so scared," he wailed. "Jesus needs to come get us!"

"David, what is the matter?" I asked.

"Jesus needs to come to get us now!" he said, waving his fork toward the field in panic. Tears spilled down his cheeks and into his bowl of applesauce.

"David, calm down," I said automatically, but I looked at the field with a fleeting thought that maybe David saw something I didn't.

"Daddy, the world is going to burn in a lake of fire, and Jesus needs to come get us now!" His palpable fear raised goose bumps on me even as I comforted him. And it was then I saw what he saw: the hill and field seemed as if they were on fire. The sunset was making it look as if the sun had begun to burn the world.

We hadn't studied the lake of fire in our family devotions, I promise. Or the Second Coming, for that matter. It wasn't on the preschool or Sunday-school agenda, either. To this day we're unsure where he learned about the Second Coming, the lake of fire or Armageddon. But David's end-time theology inspired me to self-examination. Though I was quick to comfort his fears, I later wondered if I might have undermined the seriousness with which he took God. Maybe we shouldn't be so quick to tell people not to be afraid before we find out what they're afraid of, and why.

Can you name the character trait commanded by God that nurtures respect for people and the environment? That guards against foolish behavior and is a hedge against prideful arrogance? This attribute promotes bravery, faithfulness and wholehearted devotion to God. It advances honest government, keeping those in power committed to righteousness and justice while preventing bribery, extortion and cruel behavior. People who develop it, says God, will know prosperity—good things will happen to their children. It protects people from sin. And for those who practice it God promises the protection of his angels and his watchful eye wherever they go.

Nothing could be more desirable for us today. Yet do you recognize these things as the fruit of the fear of God?

The Fear of the Lord

Fearing God is out of vogue. I cannot recall hearing a sermon on fearing the Lord in my twenty-five years of following Christ. There seems to be a certain embarrassment about it, as if someone had committed a faux pas, as if to speak of the fear of the Lord were in poor taste.

This has happened in part because our society confuses

casualness with intimacy: if you act casual with someone or something it appears that there is intimacy. This can be as unimportant as children calling elders by their first names, or as serious as casual sex. But calling people by their first names or even hopping into bed with them hardly means you know them.

Such thinking spills over to our theology. We've made God the smiling Jesus who is our buddy or boyfriend—and who would be afraid of a good buddy or boyfriend? I wince when I hear God referred to as "the big guy upstairs." It's trite and demeaning. He's not our pal; he's God. He loves you, and it's a good thing, because, make no mistake, he is terrifying to see. The fact is when those who knew him intimately came face to face with him they did not give him a punch on the arm or a kiss on the cheek. They fell on their faces—people like Abraham, Moses, Isaiah, John, Paul.

Our lack of understanding the fear of God has happened in part because we desire a softer view of God, a more palatable God for the watching world. But by losing our fear of God we gain tremendous fear of people. Everywhere I go people tell me that the thing that keeps them from sharing their faith at work, from taking a difficult stand for Christ, from being bold about their faith is fear: fear of what people will think, fear of what people will say, fear of being misunderstood, fear of what people may do. But these fears cripple our ability to live out full devotion to God. Nowadays fear of people replaces fear of God. It grips us by the throat and chokes life from the church.

What Does It Mean to Fear the Lord?

When I was a new Christian and had just started reading the Bible, I noticed that fearing God was mentioned routinely in the Old Testament and often in the New. Those around me told me that it meant "reverent respect." So that's what I believed and later taught. I remember how reverent respect seemed to be an attitude one might put on at a funeral home or during the singing of the national anthem at a baseball game. But reverent respect is only one facet of fearing God. I taught people about fearing the Lord much the same as I told David not to worry, that the world wasn't burning up. And maybe that was true, but ultimately I want to be careful not to communicate to others that God doesn't really mean what he says.

This is the fear of God: that you care more about what Jesus thinks of you than what the world thinks about you; that your concerns, thoughts, actions and behavior are geared more toward pleasing God than toward pleasing people; that what you say and do are governed more by what God wants than by what you want; that we look to Jesus to direct us, not to the world.

Jesus said it this way: "I tell you, my friends, do not be afraid of those who kill the body and after that can do no more. But I will show you whom you should fear: Fear him who, after the killing of the body, has power to throw you into hell. Yes, I tell you, fear him" (Luke 12:4-5). In other words, Jesus commands us not to fear those who even have the power to kill and, presumably, do all manner of awful things besides. Jesus tells us to fear the one who has far greater power, the one who deals with our souls: God!

As much brushing up as David's end-times doctrine might need, my concept of fearing God needs even more. David was right to worry: the world will end, if our lives don't first. One day we will meet God, the one who holds our souls in his hands. At that moment we'll want to be reverent, respectful, and much more. The Hebrew word translated "fear" could also be translated "terror." The greater part of the fear of the Lord means that we should fear him, at least when we oppose his ways, and one of the frightening things is that we are very bad at figuring out the difference between his ways and our ways.

Fearing the Lord Leads to Knowledge
Even if I was out to lunch at the dinner table, Leeann was on top of it. "David," she said, "the sun is not setting the world on fire right now, but one day Jesus will return, and we need to be ready to meet him." She continued, "David, are you ready for Jesus to come to get you?"

"No," he said.

"Would you like to be?" she asked.

"Yes."

"There's good news, David."

"What?" he said, still looking at the field but now seeing that the sun's descent behind the hill had not set the world on fire.

"If you follow Jesus and give him your life, he will never leave you, he will never forget you, he will always be with you and protect you. David, do you know what the Bible says?"

"What, Momma?"

"David, the Bible says, 'What does the LORD your God ask of you but to fear the LORD your God, to walk in all his ways, to love him, to serve the LORD your God with all your heart and with all your soul, and to observe the LORD's commands . . . ?'" (Deuteronomy 10:12).

"Okay, Momma, I'll do that," he said as he went back to eating his chicken.

3
Pint-Sized Postmodernist

Isaac, *at twenty-three* months and still too small to understand about days of the week, did begin to notice a pattern around him: pancakes meant it was Saturday, David's alarm meant a school day, everyone getting dressed in nice clothes meant a trip to the dreaded church nursery.

It was Sunday, and we were dressed and ready for church. I was sipping coffee and reading the sports section at the breakfast table when Isaac asked, "Daddy, what today?"

"Isaac," I announced brightly from behind the newspaper, "it's Sunday morning. Today we *get* to go to church." I took another sip of coffee.

"What Sunday?" he asked.

"Sunday is the first day of the week, and that's the Lord's day."

"What yesterday?"

"Well, Isaac, yesterday was Saturday, the end of the week, the Jewish sabbath."

"What today?" Isaac repeated.

"It's the Lord's day, Isaac, a day we mark for remembering the Lord's resurrection, the day he rose victorious from death and the grave. It's the Christian sabbath." I peered at him over the newspaper. I felt proud I could give these answers while still reading about the Wildcats' victory over Georgia.

Isaac, on the other hand, knitted his brow and pondered, then sighed, indicating he was singularly unimpressed. He crossed his chubby arms and leaned toward me, crushing Cheerios with his elbows. "No, Daddy," he said, "not Sunday."

"Sorry, Isaac, the fact of the matter is it's Sunday." I turned a page of the newspaper.

But Isaac had made up his mind. "It Thursday," he announced.

I set down the newspaper and looked him in the eye. I decided to drop the theological spin and come quickly to the heart of the matter. "Isaac, it's Sunday, and you're going to church."

"No-o-o-o!" he said, sticking to his guns. "It Thursday."

"Isaac, it's Sunday."

"Thursday!"

"Sunday!"

Leeann dropped a piece of toast on my plate and reminded me that I was arguing with a two-year-old. "Remember," she said with a smile, "arguing with a two-year-old is a no-win situation."

"Daddy," Isaac said firmly, "it not Sunday . . . because it Thursday—to me."

Suddenly with a flash of realization I saw this was no discussion about days of the week—or even about the nursery. This was a worldview discussion. As I stared into his unblinking eyes (so much like mine) it was clear: I was talking with a pint-sized postmodernist!

What's Your Worldview?

Sunday was Thursday indeed! Clearly Isaac rejected my story of Sunday as an oppressive metanarrative—the power play designed to force him to stay in the onerous nursery. Isaac, at his young age, had already rejected, yea, held in contempt, all critical realism!

"Hello, Michel Foucault? . . . Yes, I just called to tell you I'm seeing my son using his individual freedom to maximize pleasure, despite his mother's and my conspiracy to stifle his longing for self-expression . . . No, good heavens, no, it's not that—he's using yogurt . . . Uh-huh, yes . . . yes . . . he seems to agree with Beiner's assessment that law really does equal oppression, and decriminalization equals freedom . . . No, we won't be coming to the Anarchists' Charity Ball . . . He's got to go to the nursery—he's only two, and we're doing our best to impose the one metanarrative on him . . . Thanks . . . okay . . . yeah . . . no problem. Bye."

As I watched Isaac's relativistic expressions manifested by alternately squishing raspberry yogurt and Cheerios on top of his head, I couldn't help wondering what Leeann and I had done wrong. Did Isaac's slide down the nihilism slope come from some slip of parenting? It was almost more than we could bear.

Yet maybe, just maybe, it was nothing Leeann and I did wrong. It might be that the relativists are confused about what day it is, and they're the ones acting like Isaac rather than Isaac acting like them. Could they be the ones in an infantile revolt against God? Maybe they've designed an argument to get what they want rather than to get at the truth.

Bumper Sticker Worldview

Jim Sire in his book *The Universe Next Door* writes, "Few people have anything approaching an articulate philosophy—at least as epitomized by the great philosophers. Even fewer, I suspect, have a carefully constructed theology. But everyone has a worldview." Even children! But here's the biggest problem: In the real world most people live out unexamined worldviews. I did. It's as if I made my own worldview from clichés and bumper stickers. I tended to pick and choose the best-sounding clichés from prevailing and even conflicting worldviews. I held bits of theism when attending funerals, existentialism when looking for heroes, and naturalism when visiting the doctor. Mixed together, these "isms" give rise to a whole new worldview I call the bumper sticker worldview (BS worldview for short). Here are the basic tenets of the BS worldview: All things are relative, and there is no absolute truth, bad or good: your truth is your truth and my truth is my truth. But it is absolutely wrong if you believe in absolutes. It's bad to be moralistic or judgmental—the Bible says so. Taking religion too far is bad. A BS worldview hates self-righteous people—they're stupid. (Notice you don't have to worry about contradictions in a BS worldview.)

The BS worldview believes science is for the real world and religion is for the spiritual world, so don't mix the two. Science disproves the Bible—of course the Bible can't disprove science; it's for people with "faith." (That must mean science doesn't require faith!) Anyway, the evolutionary process has produced an amazing world. We are what we eat, we're born to shop, and polls are the greatest source of truth and morals because they're scientific.

According to the BS worldview we've advanced beyond people from yesteryear since we know lots of stuff they didn't. So don't forget that the Bible was written in another context years ago. Never mind that there's precious little new to religious or philosophical thought. And despite all evidence to the contrary, things are getting better and better. There was a poll, once, that said so.

The BS worldview believes Jesus was a great moral teacher, except for his moral teaching on money, divorce, the poor, and how we treat our neighbors. Jews, Muslims and Christians all believe the same thing—they just need to be nice to each other and realize that all religions are traveling different roads to the same mountaintop. Never mind that religious differences include heaven, hell, history, sin, prime reality and how to get to God.

Since a good God shouldn't, couldn't, won't send good people to hell, we're all going to compulsory heaven! Except Hitler and Stalin, of course . . . and the guy who cut you off in traffic last week. (Always focus on the exceptions.) The rest of us are uniquely good . . . unique just like everybody else. And since we're all good we don't need forgiveness—it's guilt that's bad. After all, we're only human. So do the best you can and be the best you can. Never mind that some are best at being racists, or raping, and some are good at cheating on taxes. (Maybe it's their truth; at least that's what Michael Foucault says.) But don't worry; God forgives. That's his job. Anything else is your parents' fault. What a great system!

The problem I had holding a BS worldview was that nagging feeling in the back of my mind that maybe this confusing mix of clichés is, well, BS. Maybe there is a God who doesn't wink at my sin. Maybe he hates my unseen pride and arrogance. Maybe he loathes my self-justification and self-right-eousness. Maybe he won't excuse my actions based on what my parents did or didn't do come Judgment Day, the day I was so quick to dismiss, the day Jesus spoke of with such confidence, the day that will come since the ultimate poll is true: one out of one dies. Hey, maybe it *is* Sunday!

Done with Bumper Sticker Worldviews

To be satisfied with a worldview that simply strings together clichés and masquerades as philosophy is dangerous for anyone who believes that Jesus spoke with any insight at all. It's a thinly veiled self-centered system to justify behavior—something any two-year-old could dream up.

But the BS worldview is a particular danger for Christians—well-meaning, goodhearted Christians—because unknowingly we become sucked into living our lives by a bumper sticker worldview that left unexamined by the light of Scripture leaves us in the dark about the spiritual reality of the world around us. Jesus said, "When you see a cloud rising in the west, immediately you say, 'It's going to rain,' and it does. And when the south wind blows, you say, 'It's going to be hot,' and it is. Hypocrites! You know how to interpret the appearance of the earth and the sky. How is it that you don't know how to interpret this present time?" (Luke 12:54-56).

I like the bumper sticker that says: "We have enough youth; how about a fountain of smart!" Face it: left to ourselves we don't want to be told what is right or wrong any more than Isaac wants to go to the nursery or I want to pay taxes. All creation is in rebellion against God. No one is good except God alone. To submit our lives to Christ means we submit our minds as well.

I want to make a plea. First to Isaac, then to anyone who

will listen. Steer clear of clichés that sound wise at first blush, and examine them in the light of Scripture. Fight against a BS worldview. Let your worldview be a gospel worldview: know it, study it, breathe it in. Be so immersed in the gospel message of Christ that it chases out conflicting, competing worldviews with its light.

As it turned out, it really was Sunday, even for Isaac. The nursery full of toys and other children convinced him. Those of us more set in our worldviews find it more difficult to change. Make no mistake: developing a gospel worldview is difficult at times, as G. K. Chesterton wrote: "It's not that Christianity has been tried and found wanting, it's that Christianity has been found difficult and left untried." But in the end it brings sight. Not one poll required.

4

Seeing
the Game

The *Los Angeles* Dodgers posted a 4-3 victory over the Cincinnati Reds. It irritated me that the Reds had the winning run on base in the eighth, then left the man stranded. Maybe that's why I felt grumpy as we made our way for the exits. Leeann felt grumpy because I barked at her for buying a cheap inflatable Reds mascot: "Good grief! You paid how much? This thing isn't worth fifty cents!" So she wasn't talking to me. It didn't help that I had to fight the crowds with the kids in tow, all for privilege of driving the sleepy ninety minutes home while the rest of the family snoozed. We were nearing the ballpark exit, and it looked as if my well-planned escape out of the parking lot to freedom just might work, when Tristan announced in a loud voice that he had to go to the bathroom—"bad."

"How bad?" I asked, scanning the area for a bush.

"Real, real bad," he said, hopping on one foot.

The line to the bathroom snaked to the upper deck, and Tristan said he wasn't sure he could make it. While I looked up the line for a parental type who might understand the urgency of cutting in line, David and Isaac got in a fight, because Isaac popped David's Reds mascot.

Isaac whined for the hundredth time that he wanted to go home. Weariness and his inflamed sense of justice prompted David to sit down on the beer-smeared concrete ramp and weep for a replacement toy. Leeann announced that no one was going to get anything if they didn't start behaving, then glared at me. It was your typical all-American, fun family outing to the ballpark.

Who would blame me for not seeing him? He's ubiquitous—that guy who sits by the gate with a cardboard message around his neck. His sign says something about how he's down on his luck and needs a job, and how he wants to work for food, and he's a vet. But he's just hustling for change, and I was hustling the kids to the car, so I didn't even think about it.

But Tristan looked him in the eye on the way past.

"Daddy, can I have a quarter?"

"No, Tristan. Move it."

"Daddy, please, can I have a quarter?"

"Tristan, I'm tired of you guys asking for stuff. Please be quiet." And he was quiet. He's a good boy.

After fighting our way out of the parking lot we started our way down Interstate 75 toward home. I finally let out my breath and said, unconvincingly, "That was fun, wasn't it, guys?" I got no response. Everyone was asleep. Except for Tristan. He was poking at his dark and contoured reflection in the side window.

"Daddy," he said, "God told me to give that man a quarter."

At first I had to piece together what he was talking about. Then I felt like justifying myself—about how it's just going for alcohol or cigarettes or something, but then my heart sank. Tristan was right. I want children who are tenderhearted to the needs they see around them, even if it means getting ripped off at times. Jesus said it was better to lose your stuff but keep your soul. Besides, I don't think we'll get to heaven and have Jesus berate us for being overly generous with poor people who beg at the gates of public places.

Ashamed, I simply said, "Oh, Tristan. I'm sorry. I'm sorry. You were right, and I was wrong." I was blind to the guy. I knew he was there, but I hadn't really seen him. I was appalled by my spiritual blindness.

There are two kinds of spiritual blindness: blindness to the spiritual reality we can't see, and worse, blindness to the spiritual reality we can see. In John 9 Jesus heals the blind beggar. It's a story of a guy who hustled for change in busy public places, maybe like our baseball stadiums. But he's not the only person blind in this chapter. I see four other types of blind people.

The Disciples

Jesus and the disciples were heading for the exits when they saw the same guy I saw at the Reds game. "Rabbi, who sinned, this man or his parents, that he was born blind?" they asked (John 9:2). Note that the disciples exhibit blindness first. Jesus treats their symptoms of blindness even before he treats the blind man (though there's no indication their cure took hold until Pentecost).

The disciples suffer from the blindness of fuzzy, culturally conditioned theology. They adopted the current cultural thinking about God. Make no mistake: they're followers of

Jesus, but they are blind to his ways. They're like so many today who are unable to articulate simple gospel theology that Jesus would have govern our lives.

Blindness from cultural theology results in a blindness to people as people. The disciples saw the blind man only as an interesting theological case study, but Jesus' response rebukes their shallowness and offers sight to them as well as to the blind man. "'Neither this man nor his parents sinned,' said Jesus, 'but this happened so that the work of God might be displayed in his life'" (John 9:3).

Imagine the anguish of the blind man's life. His society taught that his condition came as a result of sin, causing disappointment to his parents, ostracism during his childhood, futility of any hope for the future. He sat in the public square and begged. Yet Jesus saw him—truly saw him—as someone who would display the works of God.

The Neighbors

The man's neighbors are blind too. They can't see what has happened to this man. Some even say he's a different person. "His neighbors and those who had formerly seen him begging asked, 'Isn't this the same man who used to sit and beg?' Some claimed that he was. Others said, 'No, he only looks like him.' But he himself insisted, 'I am the man'" (John 9:8-9).

If your life has been touched by Jesus there will be blindness toward you as well: toward your motives, your integrity, your very identity. And what is the cure for this kind of blindness? A bold, zealous proclamation of the truth. The blind man insists to friends and family, "I am the man."

The Parents

The man's parents represent a particularly sad kind of blindness. Their blindness comes from fear of the power of the world. We shouldn't be quick to judge their timid response to the Pharisees, because the Pharisees held a frightening amount of power. It would be the same as if you received a summons for a grand jury inquiry.

" 'We know he is our son,' the parents answered, 'and we know he was born blind. But how he can see now, or who opened his eyes, we don't know. Ask him. He is of age; he will speak for himself.' His parents said this because they were afraid of the Jews, for already the Jews had decided that anyone who acknowledged that Jesus was the Christ would be put out of the synagogue" (John 9:20-22). As we look back on these parents through the lenses of time we recognize how a brave stand for their son would have made them heroes in their son's new-seeing eyes and would have placed them forever in the ranks of biblical heroes. The cure for this kind of blindness is to face and overcome our fears. As with the neighbors, we need a bold, zealous stand for Christ.

Some Christians worry about zeal. But I agree with A. W. Tozer, who said worrying about too much zeal in the church is like worrying that you're going to have to call out the riot police because there's been a major disturbance in the local cemetery. I'm all for reasonable faith, but there are times when you must let people know that the reason your life is different is because Jesus has changed you. The church needs the bold proclamation of the truth of Jesus: in the classroom, with your family, in your neighborhood and communities.

If we want people to take God seriously we must speak about God in a serious way. We must not be zany or half-cocked Christians, but Christians who are zealous because Christ has touched our lives.

The Pharisees

If the blindness of the parents is sad, the blindness of the Pharisees is disturbing. Self-righteousness moves people beyond blindness to the truth and then on to hatred of the truth. The more truth becomes apparent, the more angry they become. They stoop to wickedness by calling Jesus, the holy son of God, a sinful man. "If this man were not from God, he could do nothing," the formerly blind man tells them. To this they reply, "'You were steeped in sin at birth; how dare you lecture us!' And they threw him out" (John 9:33-34).

Phariseeism is a blindness that threatens anyone who gets a paycheck for doing Christian work: any teacher at a Christian school, any missionary, any minister. It's a danger for any Christian leader: elders, deacons, Sunday-school teachers. It's the blindness that comes from self-righteousness. The cure? There's only one: walk humbly with your God.

John Stott was asked what was the most needed thing in Christian leadership today, and he responded, unhesitatingly, "Humility." Not brains, not money, not power, but humility. If humility does not mark our Christian leadership, then it's not Christian.

The Vision for Disciples of Christ

"Jesus heard that they had thrown him out, and when he found him, he said, 'Do you believe in the Son of Man?' 'Who is he, sir?' the man asked. 'Tell me so that I may believe in him.' Jesus said, 'You have now seen him; in fact, he is the one speaking with you.' Then the man said, 'Lord, I believe,' and he worshiped him. Jesus said, 'For judgment I have come into this world, so that the blind will see and those who see will become blind'" (John 9:35-39). This man knows the Lord's touch. He has vision. There's the strength of spiritual sight in this man. He's willing to boldly proclaim Jesus' work. He fears God, not people. He's done with culturally conditioned theological wrangling; he's done with a fear of the world and the blinding pride of self-righteousness. His humble response to Jesus allows him to see Jesus as Lord. Those who gain sight display the works of God, just as Jesus promised.

Heather McCulloch, an attractive sorority girl from Tennessee, faced the same problems most of our students face when she signed up for our short-term missions program in Guatemala: raising support, spending a summer away from family, fears of illness. But Heather's biggest obstacle was blindness. Heather suffers from the eye condition know as retinitis pigmentosa, an insidious, degenerative eye disease she's had since childhood.

Heather stood at the makeshift pulpit in the only church in the village. Our weary group of fifteen sat on "pews," rough planks of wood set on cinder blocks, under the tin roof of the church. Though the day's hike took us through jungles and up mountains, Heather said she felt strong enough to share her story first. She was only a little bit scared, she said. Our attendance doubled the congregation that day. The regulars were the Ixil people—gentle Native Americans brutalized by the Guatemalan civil war. They murmured their approval as she began speaking in Spanish—with a bit of a Tennessee accent.

After greeting the congregation and mentioning how she had come to Christ at a young age, Heather explained her eye condition. Under extremely bright sunlight she has some tunnel vision, but usually she can't see much, and not at all at night. And worse, the world is gradually going dark for her. Worse still has been knowing that people greet her with a wave and a smile, and if they don't know her they think her lack of response is because she's stuck up.

"But there are things I can see better now," Heather said. "I see the Lord better. And I see the world better, for I see how many love sin more than they love God." Then she read this verse: "And if your eye causes you to sin, gouge it out and throw it away. It is better for you to enter life with one eye than to have two eyes and be thrown into the fire of hell" (Matthew 18:9).

"I understand this verse better than most people," said Heather. "Jesus knows that pulling out your eye won't stop you from sinning. He's just making it clear how much we should value the offer of his forgiveness." Then she leaned over the pulpit and asked quietly, "How much would you pay for your eyes?

"I speak with authority," she continued. "There is nothing as valuable as the salvation Jesus offers, not even your eyes." All eyes were fixed on Heather, though she could not see them. I don't know if I've ever met anyone who sees better than Heather.

A few months after we returned from Guatemala I got a letter from the missionary in the Ixil area, who reported that the little church was filled with new believers and that most of the village had come to Christ. Is there a connection? I think so. It's like God to use people who know his touch to help others see. It's like him to use people like the blind man, or Heather, or anyone who sees Jesus, to display the works of God.

So let his touch open your eyes. You never know how you may gain your sight. It might be his word of rebuke to you. It might come from someone like Heather, who can't physically see all that well. It might even come from your kid. From the Guatemalan mountains to the Cincinnati baseball diamond, Jesus' touch still opens eyes, so that we can say along with the blind man, "One thing I do know. I was blind but now I see!" (John 9:25).

Sin

*But the
L*ORD* God
called to the man,
"Where are you?"*

GENESIS 3:9

5

Calling
Your Kid

After months of planning and dreaming, we finally stood in the heart of Atlanta's inner city at a place called Glencastle. To some Glencastle looked more like a nightmare than a dream. Its thick prison walls had surrounded prisoners during Civil War days; drug addicts and vagabonds had slept in its cavelike halls in more modern times. Today, in its most recent conversion, it provides affordable housing for the working poor and space for inner-city outreach programs.

For us it served as the place to train students in overseas and home missions. Our first evening was a warm Georgia spring night. We watched the full moon rise above the Atlanta skyline. The inner city didn't seem all that scary. Sure, many of the people who lived at Glencastle were just out of jail, but they had jobs and were trying to get their lives together.

Some of us short-term missionaries would find out more about the inner city that summer through working with kids at a Christian day camp and living at Glencastle. Other teams would scatter to faraway destinations after the initial training. The students enjoyed examining each other's shiny blue passports and exotic visas for passage to places as far away as Kenya or the Ukraine. Leeann and I were leading a team to Guatemala.

We enjoy the training for these programs, since mission trips make for one long teachable moment. Perhaps it's the combination of reliance on God, earnest questions and raw panic. It proved to be an ironic time for me: I had come to teach, but through an encounter with my son, Tristan, I became the learner.

Lost

Jimmy McGee, the no-nonsense director of the Atlanta day camps, carried no romantic notions about the inner city. He informed us we needed to remember where we were. Be careful, Jimmy said. "Never, n-e-v-e-r, not ever, are any of you to go anywhere alone. You're in the 'hood."

Glencastle hummed as students prepared hearts and minds for foreign places. As I watched them I became lost in thought: *Who would become full-time missionaries? How would the world be different because they were faithful? Wouldn't it be like God to use these students to bring revival to the world!*

Thoughts of student power in world missions were lost on Tristan, however. He stayed buried in his comic books at the back of the meeting room. He displayed all the confidence of an alumni of five summer mission programs. Sometimes Tristan attended the training at Glencastle, but he most looked forward to the breaks so he could play impromptu games of whiffle ball with the students. "Tristan," we told him, "you must be good." He promised to be good. And he was—considering he was only eight years old.

Our training went well that week. Sometimes Leeann and I were able to be with Tristan, but most of the time he was bored. His books kept him busy for the first day, but on the third day I noticed he was missing as preparations were made for our evening worship. I saw his comic books lying in the back of the room. People were milling about, and the guitar players twisted the knobs on their instruments as I scanned the crowd.

"Tristan," I called. "Where are you?"

There are different kinds of calls parents make to their children. The words remain the same (except for sometimes adding the kid's middle name), but the call is different based on inflection, tone and volume. This call was the confident call. The "please come now" call.

No response.

People took their seats. The meeting was starting. My second call was the call that accents each syllable. "Tris-tan!"

The accent on each syllable is the call that says, "I'll not raise my voice, but I am serious." I wasn't worried.

Jimmy was. His face remained impassive, but his eyes and feet moved. "Trez," he called to one of the staff, "check upstairs." Trez flashed out of the room.

The group began singing, "We exalt thee . . ."

Where is he? I wondered. *Why would he wander off?* I moved with quick steps to the parking lot. "Tristan Mack Stiles!" I called. Okay, so then I was scared, and this call showed it. This call was the "you're scaring me, and you're in for it" call.

"Oh, Lord . . ." came the muffled singing.

I grabbed two staff members who were walking in late to

the meeting. "I can't find Tristan—please help me find him."

Peggy rushed to the ditch that ran by the road—she was looking into the green filth for some sign under the water. I saw Jimmy scanning beat-up cars leaving the parking lot. Raw panic. Glencastle took on the slow-motion feel of a nightmare.

"Oh, Lord," I prayed.

The final calls of a parent are tortured calls. No longer are you worried about people hearing you. Anger is gone. This is the "I'll do anything to get you back" call.

"Tristan!" I shouted. The sound of my voice, hoarse, desperate, anguished, attracted the looks of people passing by. Ignoring them I cried out again, "Tristan!"

I can't read newspapers accounts of abducted or lost children now without a lump in my throat. I can't imagine that those feelings last for days.

Only minutes passed until Trez found him, with help from some of the kind folk who lived at Glencastle. But those minutes were an eternity to me. He had wandered up to the living quarters. He just wanted another comic book, but got scared and got turned around—converted prison cell blocks all look the same.

Tristan's big fright came when he saw me, though. I'm sure I looked strange: that confusing parental look that comes with utter love, joyful relief and absolute fury. It didn't help that I dropped to my knees in the middle of the parking lot when I saw him. I wiggled my index finger at him to come, then wordlessly pointed to the ground in front of me. He knew he had been disobedient, so why was I hugging him?

The students were still singing when we got back in the meeting room. For them my eternity had lasted just fifteen minutes. Leeann began her talk as we slipped into seats in the back row, but I couldn't concentrate on the session.

Over the years I've told others to ask questions in teachable moments, and for me that moment was as teachable as they get. As we sat there I was reminded of another call for someone lost.

God's Lost Children

"Then the man and his wife heard the sound of the LORD God as he was walking in the garden in the cool of the day, and they hid from the LORD God among the trees of the garden. But the LORD God called to the man, 'Where are you?' " (Genesis 3:8-9). I'm haunted by this passage. Was God's call to Adam a progression as mine had been?

"Adam? Ad-am! *Adam!*"

I hear God's call echo, and I find I can't read this passage now without a lump forming in my throat. Losing Tristan even for moments brought a fear hard to imagine, but it was only imagined. God felt the full impact of his lost child: first in the breaking of an intimate trust relationship once shared in the Garden and replaced with fear, accusations, pain and death, and then later in the pain that came with purchasing our redemption.

Years ago I would read this passage of Genesis wondering how Adam and Eve could have done so poorly. On the surface it seems a banal sin—as silly as looking for another comic book. I've felt confident that I could have done better had I been there. But Adam and Eve's sin wasn't a memory lapse, and there's good reason none of us would have done better. Think about it: Eve was perfect. Her face unmarred by sin, her mind unmarred by sin. Her relationship with God was perfect. Don't think Eve was silly or stupid. Unlike us, she had no problems with self-image, no dysfunctions, no flaws. If you had seen her you might even be tempted to fall down and worship her.

Eve's seduction makes Satan's work more frightening and the Fall more dizzying. If one so beautiful, so brilliant, so satisfied could be seduced, so could we. If you have ever thought you would have done better in the Garden, it's only because you understand neither the power nor the cunning of Satan's seduction.

Let's look at this seduction. Satan weaves together a four-step process of seduction: doubt, distrust, deep desires and disobedience.

Doubt

"Now the serpent was more crafty than any of the wild animals the LORD God had made. He said to the woman, 'Did God really say, "You must not eat from any tree in the garden"?'" (Genesis 3:1). Satan's question is a hermeneutical question. *Hermeneutics* is a five-dollar seminary word about how we interpret the Bible. The study of hermeneutics asks the question, What did God mean by this command or that parable or this poem? It asks questions of context, language and culture. But there are two ways to ask the question. Sometimes it means "I want to know the mind of God so I can follow him." But at other times it means "How can I wiggle out of God's claims on my life?"

Well, now that you mention it, God's command does sound unreasonable, thought Eve. Tristan felt the same way. "Did Dad really mean me to stay in this building the whole time?" The more he mulled this over, the more unreasonable it seemed—in his mind—from his perspective. The same seeds of doubt are sown in our hearts daily. The naturalist tells us it's unreasonable to believe beyond what you see, so believe only in the "real world." And the materialist (a child of natu-ralism) says it's unreasonable to believe in anything you can't own, so live to shop. And the hedonist (another child of nat-uralism) says all that matters is how you feel, so if it feels good, do it.

Over time we begin to embrace these questions and doubt the clear statements of God. God says spend your time and money on things he says are important, because time and money are not your own. Neither is you body, so don't have sex with someone you're not married to. After you're married don't get divorced. Give away your faith—even if it's scary. Keep the sabbath. Let God, not your job, run your life. Trust what you can't see, not what you can.

Do these things sound unreasonable? Do they seem more like punishment than protection? Do you find yourself asking, "Did God really say . . . ?" It's the same influence Eve felt in the Garden. Unreasonable? Maybe God knows something we don't. As Oswald Chambers said, sometimes God looks like he's missing the mark because we're too shortsighted to see what he's aiming for.

Distrust

The second part of Satan's seduction comes as an interpreta-tion, not a question. And it moves Eve subtly from doubt to distrust. " 'You will not surely die,' the serpent said to the woman" (Genesis 3:4). Satan does this because he knows it's not enough for Eve to have doubts. Doubt alone does no harm. Eve must believe a lie about God before she could be seduced into an act of disobedience. So Satan tells her a whopper: "God lied to you, Eve."

It's ironic, of course, that Satan, whom Jesus called the father of lies (John 8:44), dares call God a liar. But the irony is lost on Eve. Satan even gives God's motive for lying: "For God knows that when you eat of it your eyes will be opened" (Genesis 3:5). Satan is saying, in effect, "Eve, don't you see? He's holding out on you. God lied to you because it's in his self-interest." So she believes the lie and breaks faith with God.

Attacks on God's character continue today. Today's "unreasonable" becomes tomorrow's "repressive," and doubt turns to distrust. How often science or popular culture tells us God has lied to us. The media reports with glee how scientific evidence contradicts the Bible. Heroes in the movies are those who go their own way in the face of religious structures. Theologians get front-page coverage if they question the validity of God's claims. Therapists tell us that a reason behind mental illness is a repressive church, not sin. How many times is the God of the Bible portrayed in popular media and common wisdom as the God who wants to keep you down, and that his chief pleasure is to prohibit you from experiencing the joys of life? We tend to miss the irony, just like Eve, that the life-giver would prohibit life.

With these questions all around us it doesn't take long before we think that God's reasons for us not being married to the perfect person or winning the lottery or landing the perfect job, the perfect car or the perfect children is because something is in it for God. Somehow *he* gets something out of his rules, not us.

Deep Desires

Satan's last recorded words to Eve are partially true. Lies are always more effective with a bit of truth. "You will be like God, knowing good and evil" (Genesis 3:5). The truth is that certain knowledge does come with sin. You won't just understand it's wrong to take what belongs to others, you'll know the thrill of theft. You won't just understand that illicit sex is a betrayal, you will know the exhilaration of adultery. You won't just understand it's wrong to take the life of another, you will know the power of bloodlust. Satan promises that such knowledge will be better than the ignorance God offers in innocence.

But the titillating desire to know something forbidden was not the big temptation for Eve. The main appeal of Satan's offer was to replace God by becoming God herself. To be like God was already true in part since God made her and Adam in his image. But Eve wanted more; she desired to *be* God, not just to bear his image. The appeal of this sin is a deep desire to be in charge, to run the show, to do whatever we want. A banal sin? Only in that it has universal appeal. Every time you hear someone say, "I'm going to run my life the way I want to—it's my right," you hear a declaration to be God. And it's no wonder: we're all Eve's children.

Disobedience

So Eve took the fruit and ate it. And ever since people have taken things that don't belong to them, and like Eve most would gladly trade the knowledge that comes with it for the days of innocent unknowing.

Seen clearly, our seduction happens in the same progression and with the same results as Eve's. We doubt God's word to us, we distrust his very motives in our lives and decide he really doesn't know what's best. We take things into our own hands and go our own way, only to discover we gain not the Godlike status we were promised, but fear, accusations, pain and death. We're as lost as a child in a jail.

Yet even in the midst of our despair there is hope. Our God

searches us out. One night, not long after our incident at Glencastle, Tristan asked me a question. I had just finished praying with him before bed, and as I was turning off the lights he propped up on his elbow and asked, "Daddy, why doesn't God just show up and prove to everybody that he's real?"

"Well, Tristan, that's a good question," I said. "Why do you ask?" I was only buying time to gather my thoughts. Kids' theology questions are such important breakthroughs in the routines of life.

"I was just wondering."

"Well, he did show up."

"Yeah, but not to my friends at school."

"Umm . . . yeah, I see. Tristan, you remember the story of Adam and Eve in the Garden?" I asked.

"Yeah."

"You remember how Satan lied to Eve and got her to eat the apple?"

"Dad, it wasn't an apple."

"How do you know?"

"My Sunday-school teacher read it to us, and she said it wasn't an apple."

"Okay, well, anyway, do you remember how Satan got Eve to eat the fruit of the tree of good and evil?"

"Uh-huh."

"Eve didn't have faith in God."

"So?"

"So what was broken was faith, not proof."

"So?"

"Well, I think that God wants us to have faith because it restores what was broken in the Garden."

"Hmm," he said.

"It's not proof or love or good works or anything else that was broken in the Garden—it was faith, faith in God's Word. That's why it's not love or good works that unites us to God now. It's faith. Understand?"

"I think so."

"Tristan, remember at Glencastle when you got lost?"

"Yeah." He looked down at his Mickey Mouse bed sheets.

"You remember how I came looking for you?"

"Yeah." He looked up.

"You remember how when I found you I wasn't mad, I was just glad you were okay?"

"Yeah, I really remember that."

"Not because I wanted to prove to you I was there, or to prove I was right, but because I knew you were in danger if you didn't believe my words. That's true with God too. He wants us to have faith that his ways are the best ways, even when we don't understand—not so he can prove us wrong. His concern is that we have faith in him so that we will be safe in him. You know what else, Tristan?"

"What?"

"I think God will show up to each of your friends in school in his own way and call them to himself. Just like he did for Adam and Eve."

"Just like you at Glencastle," Tristan said with a nod and a yawn. "Well, 'night, Dad."

"Sweet dreams, Tristan."

6

Dealing
with the Devil
on a Train to
Amsterdam

I *met Satan* one winter's day somewhere between the Austrian and the Swiss Alps on a train bound for Amsterdam. He came to me, as is his custom, with gentle and kind questions when I was weak. He's as reasonable and evil today as he was with Eve in the Garden of Eden.

We were returning from Africa via Europe that year, a year when we stepped out in faith to follow God's call to do missionary work in Kenya despite the risk to our newborn child. Spiritual risks bring a reward: spiritual vibrancy. Yet an exciting spiritual life doesn't mean things are comfortable—far from it. In fact a Spirit-filled life is the life most likely to encounter Satan. It's when Satan has the most to lose.

It happened to Jesus. I find this passage of Scripture the most frightening in the Bible: after the baptism of Jesus, after God pronounces his favor on Jesus and fills Jesus with his

Spirit Jesus is led by the Spirit into the desert to be tempted by Satan (Mark 1:12-13). Jesus was filled and led by the Spirit, yet was tempted by Satan!

What's your perception of how God treats those who are filled with the Spirit? Often we think that God will bless us with the right job, well-behaved kids and fat bank accounts. We sometimes think the Spirit-filled life is a life of comfort, or worse, a life that makes God do things the way we want him to, like he's our celestial butler. But if the Spirit led the Son of God into the desert rather than into abundance on earth, if the Spirit led Jesus to be tempted by Satan in the desert when Jesus was filled with the Spirit, then we should know that if we walk with the Spirit we will walk in the desert too.

Led to a Train Bound for Amsterdam

As our train sped away from Vienna the outside winter temperature plummeted below zero; inside the air became hot and brittle. Running my hand across the seat covers raised a cloud of dust that set Tristan wheezing. As we crossed the German border Tristan began to struggle for breath—it was asthma, but we didn't think asthma was all that dangerous. As snow-capped chalets whizzed by our train window the conductor said we were hours away from the closest hospital. That's okay, we said, it's only asthma.

At first Tristan fought for breath, but over time he began to grow weak. Leeann and I realized it was much more serious than we had first thought. Tristan bleated out each breath with a labored, raspy sound. His small chest heaved with each breath and his eyes rolled at us in fear, as if asking for help. We began to plead with God.

What started as open and tearful requests—"Oh God, please heal my son"—over the next number of hours became clenched teeth and clenched-fist demands: "God, heal Tristan—*now!*" That's when Satan meet me. My son was dying, my thinking was jumbled. I felt panicked and scared, something Satan finds most to his liking. His arrival in our cabin was unannounced, except for a chill in the room. I'm not sure how long he sat next to me until he spoke. I do know that Leeann didn't move from her position of hovering over Tristan, tears dripping on his small body.

"Mack, let's reason together," he said. It was as if someone had turned off the sound of the clicky-clack, clicky-clack of the train wheels and Tristan's cries. It was an angelic voice, one of calm in the midst of panic and fear. He was an angel once; he can still play the part.

"You didn't really think God had the time, did you? We can't be overly sentimental about these things," he said kindly. "God's holy, and, quite frankly, you're much too . . . disappointing, you know. You and your baby. Really, if you think about it, you're only getting what you deserve." It was a fatherly voice breaking bad news of a belief in Santa Claus that's gone on a bit too long.

"Mack," he continued, "Mack, don't forget—God abandoned his own Son. What makes you think he'll be here for you when you need him in your sorrow?" It seemed such a hard, reasonable truth. How could God possibly love me with all my failing and weaknesses? My sins seemed too present and large for a holy God. My concerns for a tiny baby seemed microscopic compared to the concerns of the kingdom of God. Lies are always more forceful when mixed with truth.

Then came Satan's temptation: "He's abandoned you, Mack. Curse him. Curse God."

I stood on the brink. A friendly voice was tempting me in my despair and at my greatest point of weakness. But I had something Eve did not: Christ's finished work on the cross and the indwelling of the Holy Spirit. Yes, God promised pain, but he also promised he'd never leave me or forsake me.

"Go away," I whispered.

Leeann turned to me. "What?"

I felt as if I were surfacing from a dream. I shook my head and said, "I'm going to have my quiet time."

"You're going to do what?" she said, incredulous.

"I'll explain later. I'm going to have my quiet time. I need to talk to Jesus."

While Tristan gasped for breath I poured out my heart to God. I still have my journal from that trip. It's beat up and tattered, but the words are fresh. Here's how it reads.

March 3: The worst day of my life. I've never faced a crisis of faith like this. Tristan struggles for every breath, and I'm not sure he'll make it, but Lord, I serve you. Lord, I follow you.

Within moments of writing those words we lurched into the Zurich station. Events blur. I remember the police helping us. I remember watching the train leaving for Amsterdam with all our luggage (and not caring). I remember the distress and fear of our taxi driver as he raced us across town to the children's hospital. I held Tristan in the back seat and rocked him and whispered, "Hold on, little guy, hold on." His eyes rolled to the back of his head. His fingers and lips were blue as we ran into the emergency room. I remember the ordered mayhem of the *Kinderspital* emergency room and the Swiss efficiency as nurses and a doctor attended to our son. Within minutes of his breathing treatments he gasped, coughed up phlegm and sputtered for breath, but air began to fill his lungs—sweet air. We felt as if we had been vomited up on shore like Jonah.

That hospital, one of the best in all Europe, was the place

the Spirit was rushing us to all along, of course. Not only for Tristan but for me as well. The week we spent in that hospital became a place for Tristan's recovery and for my reflection.

Malice and the Evil One

There's another journal entry for the next day written on bits of notebook paper taped into my journal (since my journal made its way to Amsterdam with the luggage).

> March 4: It's dawning on me that I did not imagine a visit from the evil one. Satan really came to me yesterday on the train.

I remember a time when I was agnostic about Satan, at least the cartoon version of Satan: red tights, pitchfork, goatee, horns. I still don't believe in that, but I do believe Satan is a personal evil force so filled with malice for God and his children that he would sift us all like sand through his sieve of hatred—even little children like Tristan—if he could. The empirical evidence for an evil force in the world seems hard to ignore, and besides, I've met him and have given up my agnosticism.

Yet I'm still no expert, and I don't care to be much of one. As C. S. Lewis noted, there are two mistakes Christians can make about Satan: to pay him too much attention, or too little. Today I think I understand enough: Satan's chief power in the world is to tempt people to think and do evil. The rest of his power is chaff compared to that. It doesn't take many looks at the condition of the world to say this power is power enough. It's no wonder Jesus taught us to pray that God would "lead us not into temptation, but deliver us from the evil one" (Matthew 6:13). For us to give in to Satan's lies and temptations is how he wins in our lives and in the world.

Greater Is He . . .

The biggest lesson for me was not about Satan at all, but about God and his love.

> March 5: The Lord told me today he counted every hair on my head. He told me he is never too busy for me. He reminded me that my sins and faults and failures were never too big for him.

After all the kindness God has shown me in my life, how I could miss his love? Is my faith so thin I would turn against him at the first brush with danger? Well, yes. That's the depth of our sinfulness and why we so desperately need a Savior.

> I was reminded today by the Lord, gently, of his love, not just for me but for Tristan. He reminded me he loves Tristan even more than I, something hard to imagine, but true.

I've found it helpful to remind myself that God loves those around me, but I find it especially helpful to remind myself that God loves those I love more than I do or ever will.

Tristan's recovery overjoyed us; yet as he improved we began to notice the collective anguish in the rooms by ours. The child next to us had just gone through open-heart surgery. The child on the other side battled leukemia. I felt embarrassed and overwhelmed that we were even there.

We watched the children's and parents' pain intimately, and they ours, since the upper half of the walls in the rooms were made of glass. It provided a God's-eye view of collective pain. Some parents held the hands of their children, some wept, others prayed. In some rooms there were frantic movements of nurses and doctors, while in other rooms someone read a book. These eerie juxtapositions of action and stillness were made all the more eerie by the absolute silence of the rooms. As I looked down the row of rooms it gave me the sensation that I was peering through water. The last rooms on either end of the row of rooms were murky and dark green because of the thickness of the glass panes. In every room there was a story of a child and a frightened parent or two. Children died there. Never had the phrase "Makes you wonder if there's a God, doesn't it?" seemed so applicable. *Why did they lose their child and we didn't?* I wondered.

The Great Comforter

March 6: The Lord reminded me that not one story here is murky to him. He knows what it's like to lose a son. To what God would we flee in our pain but the God who lost a child? The Lord reminded me too that he is acquainted with pain and suffering. They called him a man of sorrow, and he reminded me that from his sorrow has come great joy, much like Tristan's name. (*Tristan* means "out of sorrow comes a shout of joy.")

Of course the astute reader notices that God didn't answer my question directly. It's like God to answer indirectly. Just look at the conversations in the Bible. What he does do is point to himself: the God who goes with us even in our pain. I find, with time, those answers more satisfying, given the complexities of life.

I don't remember how we took pictures in the Zurich hospital. Maybe Leeann's camera came with us in her purse. One of the shots shows Tristan, surrounded by tubes connected to his breathing apparatus, playing peekaboo though the stainless-steel bars of his crib. He seemed secure in our love for him. He knew he was watched over and cared for. And I knew I was too.

7

For the Love of Trinkets

I *fault Tristan's* grandparents—my parents—for our miserable drive to Florida to see my sister. Of course they meant well. They were only being generous when they gave Tristan ten dollars for the spring-break trip. But it was more money than he had seen before. It was more money than he could handle.

"Ten dollars!" he exclaimed as the green bill fluttered out of the envelope onto the floor. "Wow!" Leeann picked the Easter card off the table and read it, but only to herself. Tristan's newfound wealth brought temporary deafness.

I didn't notice the fever pitch of his covetousness until we stopped for gas a few minutes into our fourteen-hour trip. "Dad, can I get this?" Tristan held up a pair of plastic eyeglasses with plastic eyeballs attached to springs. "It's only $3.95!"

And you thought ten dollars wouldn't buy much anymore.

The number of goods under ten dollars is phenomenal, and Tristan pondered purchasing all of them: from Slim Jim beef jerky to inflatable palm trees, from drinks in every conceivable container to day-old donuts, from plastic birds that dip and drink from your coffee cup to candy that whistled. But wait—there's more. It's not just goods, but services. He found slots to deposit quarters in at every turn: video games, fiberglass animals that jerk back and forth, and claws that grab for stuffed animals in glass booths.

Explaining to a four-year-old Tristan that "if you put your quarter into the machine you can't get it out" was reason enough for him not to play a video game. At six this sort of logic brought an exasperated "Oh, come on, Daddy." But now at seven and with his own money, any reason became as disposable as a bubble-gum wrapper.

Driving time became mere intermissions between roaming the aisles filled with things to buy. Midway though our trip I wondered if all those eighteen wheelers were carrying only trinkets and video games to highway rest areas. We promised Tristan that if he could just hang on for a few more hours he could buy some of the same stuff in Florida, but in Florida it would have "Florida" printed on it. But I think the real reason his ten dollars remained unspent resulted from the overwhelming choices.

Our late-night arrival in Tampa meant carrying the children to my sister's upstairs condo, and while I tucked Tristan in on the foldout couch he muttered, "I think I'll get the slingshot."

The next morning was Easter, and though we were tired from the day of driving we felt we needed to go to church.

"Ginny, what's the closest church?"

My sister smiled at my lack of denominational concern and said, "Well, for this week a big church, Idlewild Baptist, has rented the Sun Dome, and they're having church there."

"That'll do," I said.

Since it was Easter Sunday, the service started an hour earlier than usual, so we missed most of it. But after we arrived and were finally able to sit, I did notice Tristan listening to the pastor with unusual attention. Then the choir crescendoed, and the Kentucky Fried Chicken buckets appeared: the offering. It was to be the only part of the service we saw in its entirety.

I felt miffed and ripped off. I wanted to worship the Lord on Easter. I looked at Leeann, and she looked back, but her eyes were shining. She wordlessly directed my gaze to Tristan. Tristan had reached into his pocket and pulled out the object of his longings and lust and covetousness and was staring at the crumpled-up wad of his ten-dollar bill. Tristan looked as if he were the only person in that building carrying on a conversation in his inner heart.

It dawned on me that we were at Idlewild Baptist Church for another reason than for me to get blessed. It was God who set up that fourteen-hour drive to bring us to that very spot. Jesus was knocking on Tristan's heart. After all, covetousness is a sin if you're seven or seventy, carnal or cute.

Leeann's head went down in prayer. I did the same. When I handed Tristan the bucket I noticed his hands shook. Tristan held the ten-dollar bill over the bucket, then jerked back his hand as if he'd touched something hot, then slowly he put his hand out again and dunked it. The wadded-up bill thumped against the empty bottom of the bucket. I felt as if it had been the game-winning shot. Leeann and I almost rose up with a cheer and high fives. It was the most exciting offertory in my life.

Of course the one who least realized what had happened

was Tristan. He did not know that for that one act I would have gladly bought every magnetic alligator with "Florida" printed on it, every bag of Gummi worms, every M & M, every bag of marbles, every bottle, bouncy ball and slingshot from Tampa to Canada. But the amazing thing, after our time with the good Baptist folk at Idlewild, was how little he seemed to want that stuff on the way home. There was no more fantasizing about worthless trinkets; we enjoyed conversation. Tristan even took time to sit back and delight in the ride. Amazing. But then, we shouldn't be amazed. That's how it is with God. When we give away our stuff, God gives us something back—something better than more stuff: freedom from things.

Having Money: The Same as Loving It?

I used to say money is neither good nor bad; it is just an amoral instrument. Used correctly, it's beneficial; used wrongly, it does harm. But the famous French theologian Jacques Ellul argued persuasively that money is more than amoral; it actually contains inherent spiritual power. That's why Jesus said, "You cannot serve both God and Money" (Matthew 6:24). And Jacques Ellul notes that the way to profane the idol of money is to treat it as if it's unimportant by giving it away. When we do, our hearts are released from the power of money.

Years ago I thought it was simple: if you were wealthy you were not on Jesus' side. Jesus would not own a BMW. The problems of the poor were simple too. Excessive American consumption fostered the problems of the poor worldwide. If we just spread around our stuff and lived more simply, there wouldn't be any poor. Share lawn mowers in your neighborhood, and don't eat grain-fed beef.

But two problems arose with my understanding of the

world: I met the rich and poor. I don't just mean the well off; I'm talking rich. My work with a "faith ministry" required that I raise support. Sometimes support comes from people who deal with sums of money unimaginable to most Americans, certainly to me. I found some of these people quietly give 80 to 90 percent of their wealth away. One couple told me that they give one million dollars away—every year—and said they were committed to continue as long as God prospers their business. That's a million a year they could use for themselves. And they're down-to-earth people who live a middle-class lifestyle. They don't drive a BMW, but if they did I would not point fingers, because who they are forces me to wonder if I would be as generous. I've come to see that Jesus is more concerned about the generosity of a person's heart than the price of their car.

The Poorest Poor

I've met the poor too. Part of the money I raise is for missions work. Over the last decade our family has spent most of our summers working with missionaries who work with the poor, people so poor my tongue and pen do injustice to their poverty.

Our latest work took place in the Ixil triangle of Guatemala at a clinic for malnourished children. We have snapshots of Tristan gently cradling a little slip of humanity named Juana. She was two years old and weighed just under ten pounds. Despite the love and good food she received at the clinic, she died of complications from malnourishment two weeks after her arrival. Her father's anguish pierced me. But it's a common story at the clinic.

Deaths such as Juana's are difficult to explain to my children. I'm more unsure today as to why Juana died. The truly astonishing fact is that there was plenty of food available in the Ixil triangle when she died.

I long to make a difference for the poor. I will still take my family to live with the poor despite the dangers. I still don't eat grain-fed beef. But my old thoughts about the rich and the poor just don't work. I do know I've come to hate the clichés about both rich and poor. They focus on others rather than ourselves. Clichés elevate and insulate us from seeing our own poverty by pointing our fingers at someone else. Besides, clichés and stereotypes cut both ways.

Spiritual Richness in Poverty

I remember sitting on a street curb in Nairobi with Ken, a Stanford student. We had just returned from an area of northern Kenya where he served a Kenyan pastor in his home. We talked about how little the pastor owned, the dirt floor, the outhouse, the hand-to-mouth existence. Yet Ken marveled at the joy of his home, the vibrancy of his ministry, the amazing generosity of the family.

"Mack," he said, "there's a richness to that place we are blind to. There's a big difference between being impoverished and being in poverty." He looked across the street at the wealthy tourists getting into safari vans for their tours of game parks—completely isolated from the real richness of the Kenyan culture.

Ken commented, "Those tourists look happy." He paused, smiling. "And they don't know any different!" We looked at each other and roared at his twist of an old cliché.

Jesus understood how to twist clichés too. He said to the church in Laodicea, "You say, 'I am rich; I have acquired wealth and do not need a thing.' But you do not realize that you are wretched, pitiful, poor, blind and naked. I counsel you to buy from me gold refined in the fire, so you can become rich; and white clothes to wear, so you can cover your shameful nakedness; and salve to put on your eyes, so you can see" (Revelation 3:17-18).

Buying Ultimate Possessions from Jesus

Wealth blinds us to our own impoverishment. The way out is in our response to Jesus, not in pointing our fingers at the rich or wringing our hands about the poor. Our freedom comes by buying from God long-term investments, clothes for godly adornment and medicine for healing our blindness. How? After Jesus tells the Laodiceans of their poverty he says, "Those whom I love I rebuke and discipline. So be earnest, and repent. Here I am! I stand at the door and knock. If anyone hears my voice and opens the door, I will come in and eat with him, and he with me" (Revelation 3:19-20).

For years I thought this was a verse on evangelism. Nope. It's a verse for Christians to respond to Christ's call about your wealth. It's about the way to kill covetousness and develop a generous heart. It's the way to know true wealth by taking Christ into your life, completely, fully, wholeheartedly, so that you can dunk your stuff. Then you'll know the same freedom Tristan did on the ride back from Florida: no more fantasizing about trinkets, but instead deeper conversations with God and the freedom to delight in the ride.

8

TV Idols

Idols. *Shaped* by human hands, they have enigmatic life all their own. An idol mysteriously begins to control its very creator. Its power and aura grow as it is worshiped by the adoring masses. Especially when it's beaming some sporting event direct to our living room. While carved figures present idolatrous temptation to some, TV promotes idolatry around the globe. If people from yesteryear could see us sitting open-mouthed in front of these boxes playing the NCAA college tournament into our living rooms, they might think we were worshiping them.

Then comes the commercial. "Gillette! The Best a Man Can Get" goes the catchy refrain during halftime of the Final Four. A leggy, half-naked woman jumps into a handsome man's arms. He swings her around in slow motion. They embrace. She helps him apply shaving cream.

It's amazing how something as mundane and boring as shaving can be so primal, so sexy. I see few parallels in my sad-eyed, sleepy ritual every morning. Leeann shows no interest in smearing shaving cream on my face, and though the boys like to watch me shave on occasion, they gawk more than admire. I use Gillette, but it doesn't help. It's just an image on TV.

I wouldn't have even noticed the theological implications of the ad if Tristan hadn't pointed it out. "Dad, I thought Jesus was the best a man could get."

At first I thought he was making a joke, but cynicism never crossed his mind. His honest puzzlement, an outgrowth of his childlike perspective, sprang from a sincere heart.

We expect ads to lie. Tristan doesn't—at least not yet. Not long before the Final Four he ripped open a box of Toasted Chocolate Marshmallow Rainbow Oats, which he bought with his own money and a month's worth of nagging. "This stuff tastes yucky," he snorted. "And the toy broke when I took it out of the bag!" He frowned indignantly at the cheap plastic parts held in his cupped hand while the colors of the cereal bled together to form a gray mush.

What Did You Expect from an Idol?

When the people saw that Moses was so long in coming down from the mountain, they gathered around Aaron and said, "Come, make us gods who will go before us. As for this fellow Moses who brought us up out of Egypt, we don't know what has happened to him." Aaron answered them, "Take off the gold earrings that your wives, your sons and your daughters are wearing, and bring them to me." So all the people took off their earrings and brought them to Aaron. He took what they handed him and made it into an idol cast in the shape of a calf, fashioning it with a tool. Then they said, "These are your gods, O Israel, who brought you up out of Egypt." (Exodus 32:1-4)

You've gotta hand it to Aaron: he's resourceful. Never mind that the people are talking about his brother—he's threatened with mob violence and hints of a coup. So he gives them what they want: a familiar god, one made of gold that plays host deity for an orgy the following day.

I've been tempted to write off Israel's scourge of idolatry as a problem of primitives. Besides, their idols have no bearing on my life today. Idol worship seems hopelessly out of date, as silly as worrying about the theological implication of buggy whips. I even own a real idol, one I brought back from Africa. I'm as tempted to worship it as I am to eat my dog's dinner. Yet idolatry is alive and well on planet Earth—only its form has changed. Here are five reasons why.

The Allure of False Promises

The idols of Israel were akin to Toasted Chocolate Marshmallow Rainbow Oats: widely promoted, bad taste. They promised healthy crops and potent animals—never mind that they never delivered. Idols took God's goodness and claimed it as their own, so the people were duped year after year. The plague of idols lasted for millennia. Fertility rites and idols were bedfellows in the agricultural society's version of the get-rich-quick scheme.

But we're not much different. Modern-day idols still make promises to meet needs quicker, better, faster than doing things biblically—especially the idols that claim to be biblical. I'm constantly astounded, even embarrassed, by the ads I hear on Christian radio: "Quack pills guaranteed to bring your friends true love while you get rich—Pastor Jimmy Bob says so." "Use our program for your kids, and we guarantee they'll turn out godly." Christians have an amazing capacity to believe and promote false promises and then beg for more. We desperately want to believe false promises, because they offer good things—but take worldly shortcuts to get there.

This facet of idolatry springs from our dissatisfaction with the promises of God. He makes fewer promises about what we'll get and more about how we can know him.

The Draw of Tangibility

We tend to believe the cliché "The camera never lies." But the statement "The camera always lies" is closer to the truth. Cameras create images, not reality. The allure of TV is that it creates an image that seems alive or true. Idols do the same. And since images of God always lie, God forbids them.

Fright and insecurity drove the children of Israel to Aaron, who knew that the most assuring image was one they could see and touch and perhaps even remember from Egypt. We can hardly blame them for wanting security. They experienced unimagined dangers far from home, and this Jehovah God was scary. The allure for a tangible, tame God is only natural.

We too want the kind of security we can see and touch. We want our retirements to be secure, our kids to be moral, our worship of God to be unaltered week after week. Most of all, we don't want a God who's scary. But when we serve a safe God we worship only an image, a representation, a part of God, not the real thing. This idolatry springs from our dissatisfaction in the security God offers—because often it doesn't seem that secure.

The Luster of Gold

Aaron and the Israelites wanted the things of God to be inherently valuable, not contained in hidden value.

To make a god of gold is to make a god who values the things we value. Every time we rally around celebrity Christians rather than faithful Christians we tell people that Christianity is worthwhile not for who God is, but for how great we are. We are trading God's glory for plastic toys—a cheap, but effective, idolatrous ploy.

This is unfortunate, since the biblical God is very uninterested in what we value. In fact he seems to take delight in coming to us in mangers and on donkeys, in choosing the least of the least and those who are lowly, in presenting himself as a God of the weak and broken and downtrodden and marginalized. When we are dissatisfied with the things God values, we begin to worship something other than God, something only we value.

The Attraction of Sex

Fertility religions and Madison Avenue both know that sex sells. Sex gets our attention and keeps us coming back for more. Idols promised to be the best a man could get in Israel— lots of sex in fertility rites. But, like shaving cream, it's mostly just air and empty ritual. Ritual prostitution only aped the love that comes from hammering out commitment over years.

The lure of easy sex in our culture is as old as the Bible. It draws us to idolatry, it says pleasure is the best you can get. But the Bible plainly says that those who worship idols will become like them. Is there any wonder why those who sacrifice commitment at the feet of sex become unable to trust or stick with commitments?

The Pull of Self-Service

Often I hear the phrase *"My* God wouldn't _____!" (Insert

theological retort, such as "send a good person to hell" or "let bad things happen to good people," usually stated with righteous indignation.) Such phrases make me think of Aaron, who proved adept in manufacturing a god for popular opinion. John Calvin said it this way: "The human heart is an endless factory for the production of idols." Be careful what *your God* does or doesn't do. This desire to have God think like us is often only the desire to make a God in our own image.

The evangelical community is in danger of worshiping this idol. I hear it in the subtle shift from wanting God to bring revival so that I will have the opportunity to share in his love and know his glory, to wanting a God who brings revival so that my kids won't be threatened by a pagan environment. Quite suddenly we discover we are worshiping a different God from the God of the Bible. This desire for God to serve us rather than for us to serve God is idolatry.

Seeing Modern Idols—The Beginning of a Cure

Our problem is not whether or not idols exist—they surround us as water covers fish. Our problem is that they are hard to see, as hard as Tristan's recognizing bad cereal or my seeing idolatry in a shaving-cream commercial. So punch the power button on the remote, or just throw the stupid thing out the window. Ask yourself this question: In what ways are you dissatisfied with how God is running things? If you can identify your dissatisfaction with how God is running the show, you can identify the place where you are tempted for idols to become your god.

Perhaps you feel abandoned ("we don't know where this fellow has gone"), or maybe your dissatisfaction is with the demands God makes on your life. Are your kids not who you want them to be? Maybe you feel God is not making enough effort to meet your needs. Maybe you think he wants you to risk more than you can bear.

Often actions betray dissatisfactions. Sure, we can go shopping or play sports or see movies on the sabbath because we're free in Christ, but do you ever carve out time for quiet? Do you really work that hard because your job is a ministry? Maybe you value success more than God does. Casual sexual attitudes might be progressive, but they also might be creeping into your life because you've been seduced by the world's sexual values. Do you disparage your parents in the name of psychological healing, or just because you want to blame someone else? If ads lie to us, what wrong could there be if we stretch the truth?

Eighty percent of the battle is won when we can see the idols in our lives, but don't stop there. No healing happens without action. It's not good enough to just see diseases; we need to cut them out. We need to be healed by focusing on these words: "Since, then, you have been raised with Christ, set your hearts on things above, where Christ is seated at the right hand of God. Set your minds on things above, not on earthly things. For you died, and your life is now hidden with Christ in God. When Christ, who is your life, appears, then you also will appear with him in glory. Put to death, therefore, whatever belongs to your earthly nature: sexual immorality, impurity, lust, evil desires and greed, which is idolatry" (Colossians 3:1-5). Paul tells us to put our hearts on things above, with Christ, and one day we'll be glad we did when Christ appears. Then Paul lists many of the same things we see in Aaron's folly: evil desires (from false promises), greed (the lure of gold), sexual immorality, and more.

Kill the idols in your life by making Christ your life. We, the Christian community, must find our satisfaction in God and

God alone. As Jonathan Edwards said, "God is most glorified by us when we are most satisfied in Him." If we practiced that, our problems with idolatry would be over. Or, as a more contemporary theologian, Tristan Stiles, said, "The best someone can get is Jesus, and nothing in the world can compare to him. Right, Dad?"

"Right, Tristan."

Grace

*So he got up
and went to his father.
But while he was
still a long way off,
his father saw him
and was filled with
compassion for him;
he ran to his son,
threw his arms around
him and kissed him.*

LUKE 15:20

9

Brotherly Birthday Parties

David's mild learning disability makes normal interactions difficult. He wants friends desperately, but he doesn't know how to make them, so he plays by himself. David's the child on the edge of the playground, absorbed in his pretend game while other kids play kickball. David's saintly teachers say he's "hard to reach" or "distant." We say he's wonderful—sweet natured, big hearted and innocent. Of course that's the pain of it: his big heart and innocent spirit make it hard for us to watch him get picked on while riding the school bus. A child's world can be surprisingly cruel to those who are different.

I have learned not only about God's sight by watching my children. I've learned also about his joy.

We were sitting around the dinner table when Isaac began a favorite topic—birthdays. He announced there were 153 days until his sixth birthday. He then rattled off the invited guests.

I have only one birthday every four years (February 29), and Tristan loves that he's catching up with me. "On my next birthday I'll have more birthdays than Dad!" he said.

Isaac and Tristan bantered good-naturedly about how many birthday parties they've been invited to. I laughed and looked at Leeann, who was looking at David. Her nose was twisted into the funny shape it gets when she's holding back tears.

David was pushing his macaroni and cheese from one side of the plate to the other. "What's up, David?" I asked. (I don't have that mother's sense.)

"Bill said he was going to invite me to his party," David said, a bit too loudly, the way he does when he's being brave. David had been telling us for months about Bill's party.

David continued, "But then when I heard he had it last week I asked him why I couldn't come, and he told me that the reason he didn't have me after all was because he had to take his little brother, and he didn't have enough space for me after he'd asked all the other guys at our table."

"I'm sorry, David," I said.

The talk around the meal turned to silence. David doesn't usually go to birthday parties, so Bill's had been talked about with almost daily anticipation.

Tristan sat frozen in his seat as he realized what was going on. He imagined David's embarrassment. He loves his brother and is filled with compassion for him. He gets asked to birthday parties routinely and would gladly give David one of his spots.

David kept pushing his noodles around his plate. Now tears made their way down Leeann's face. It's not a birthday party that gets her, it's the sense of seeing a little guy beaten down with constant reminders that he's different. Leeann worries about how he's going to make it when the world gets crueler and harder.

My reaction is the most unhelpful of all. I'm having a fantasy of searching the halls of Maxwell Elementary for Bill so I can grab him by the lapels and shake him like a rat. "Why didn't you invite my kid to your birthday party, you little . . . ?"

David still looked down at his macaroni and cheese and repeated, "He didn't have enough space."

It was Isaac, just five years old, who responded sensibly. "Well, David," he said, "you can come to my birthday party."

"Really?" said David, brightening up.

"Yeah," said Isaac. "We'll have a great time."

"Cool!" said David.

Tristan found his voice and stabbed the air with his fork. "Yeah, David, you can come to my party too!"

"Thanks, Tristan," said David.

Leeann brightened and croaked out, "And I want you to come to my party, David."

I added my invitation to the others, and Leeann mentioned that Jesus had the biggest party of all planned, and we were all invited to that too.

Right there David had five invitations. Never mind that we only repeated standing invitations. Never mind that Leeann's birthday isn't going to be at Lazer Tag, or that my next birthday wouldn't be for years. For that matter, it was 153 days before Isaac's birthday (a childhood millennium). But never mind all that. It was enough that David knew he was loved.

God's Family

My heart was filled with thankfulness and joy for Isaac's response. Isaac unashamedly loved and cared for his brother. He was unashamedly proud to have his brother come to his party. Isaac's great-hearted response to his hurting brother showed me I don't have to have all the answers. I don't need to be David's public defender. I need to respond with the kind of love Isaac showed around our table: spontaneous, authentic, helpful.

Those in the family of God—the church—need the same: authentic, loving, helpful responses to those who are hurting or lonely or weak. You think my heart warmed at Isaac's love for his brother? "Both the one who makes men holy and those who are made holy are of the same family. So Jesus is not ashamed to call them brothers" (Hebrews 2:11). Jesus makes believers into a family. This family is a family Jesus identifies himself with proudly.

Think of God's response to love between brothers and sisters in the family of God. Think of the joy of the Father when brothers and sisters rejoice with one another. Think of the pleasure of the Father when needs are met, a thoughtful word is said, when invitations to parties are given. Especially when love is given to those of the family who may be difficult to love.

Think of the joy of the Father when our love cuts across barriers, divides and differences, when the love we have for each other overcomes what others might think about us, what those outside the family might say, or even what we ourselves might feel.

How much desire does the Father have for the church to love one another in this way? I knew just a hint of it when I watched Isaac love his brother. For if the father feels the pain of his children more intensely, doesn't he feel the joy more intensely too? Make joy in heaven, love a brother or sister across the barriers. Love them if they're awkward, or shy or hurting. Issue invitations, lots of them. Don't be ashamed, just as Jesus is not ashamed to call us brothers and sisters, and then revel in the Father's joy.

10

The Second Time
at Second Grade

David and I were having an ice cream cone on the back porch after David's second day of second grade.

"Did you make any new friends?" I asked tentatively.

"Yes," David said unexpectedly, but he looked stoic.

"That's great news, David," I said with genuine joy. "What's his name?" I tried not to act too surprised.

"He didn't tell me his name."

"How did you make a friend with someone who didn't tell you his name?"

David took a bite of ice cream, then cone. "Well, this boy on the playground at recess asked me if I wanted to be friends, and I said 'Sure!' But after we talked some he ran over to the other kids and started shouting, 'He did fail, he did fail, he did fail!'"

David wouldn't look up at me. He licked the chocolate ice

cream dripping off his fingers. Then he stopped and stared down at the drippings on the ground. "Why did he do that, Daddy?" he asked quietly.

All I could get out was, "I don't know, David."

"He doesn't really want to be my friend, does he, Daddy?"

"I don't think so, David." My voice betrayed my anguish. David looked up and studied me with his big brown eyes. Maybe I looked as ripped up on the outside as I did on the inside from this cruelest of blows. David put his hand on my arm. He deals with psychological sucker punches better than his dad, so he wanted to help.

"Don't worry, Daddy. Some other boys stopped him before everyone in the class heard."

I didn't know how to tell him I didn't care what the other kids knew about him. I wanted to tell him I'd rather have a son who repeated second grade a thousand times than a son who made fun of kids who did. I wanted to tell him this was our nightmare in holding him back in school. I wanted to tell him how much I hated that he had to go though a hard time when he was only eight and his heart was bigger than most grownups'.

"David, you didn't fail," I said weakly. "You're just trying again. You only fail when you quit."

"Yeah," he said.

We both knew this doesn't help much in the face of taunts from classmates.

"Dad?"

"Yes, David."

"I got chocolate on your arm."

"I know, David. It's okay."

A Hard Start

Life started out hard for David. At the very beginning we were just glad he was alive. His skull, fractured from his traumatic delivery, required weeks to heal. Most parents are delighted if their infant sleeps, but we had to wake David even to feed him, and it frightened us. Though his fractured skull healed and his sleep patterns became normal, Leeann felt something wasn't right.

Things took an about face when David turned five. Doctors gave us a crushing diagnosis: David was autistic. Autism is a life sentence to affected speech, extreme self-absorption and detachment from reality. We prepared the best we could. We loved him all the more.

A year later things took another turn. The doctors decided it was all a mistake and had the diagnosis overturned: David exhibited mild learning disabilities, and he might struggle in school, but he would be fine—socially awkward at times, and in need of speech therapy, but fine. Through it all we loved David all the more.

I've asked God some tough questions about David, and he answered with this Scripture: "In bringing many sons to glory, it was fitting that God, for whom and through whom everything exists, should make the author of their salvation perfect through suffering" (Hebrews 2:10).

Our salvation was made perfect though Jesus' sufferings! And his heavenly Father watched. My attention and watchfulness over David's small sufferings couldn't begin to compare to the attention and watchfulness of God toward his Son. The implications of God's commitment to enter into our suffering boggles my mind. God the Father, the one who counts hairs on heads and knows the sparrows that fall, saw every painful thing his child faced. He heard every taunt, curse and word of hatred. He felt the shame of his Son's arrest as a common criminal. He felt the pain of watching his child beaten, bloodied and, barely alive, hung on a tree. I imagine God the Father wincing with each cry of pain. He heard the pleas of his Son for his help, he saw his Son's trust, yet he knew he could not be there when his Son needed him the most. I have no doubt that this was the Father's greatest pain. Not the humiliation and shame of his Son before the taunting crowds, nor even the spear or nails that pierced him, but watching his Son agonize alone.

If I were God, it would not be this way. If I were God I would make sure that everyone knew my son's loving heart and my fearful wrath to those who hurt him. His peace and comfort would be my goal. My son would be insulated from the world's cruelty. If I were God, my son could not be hurt. I would never abandon my son. But I'm not God, and it's a good thing. Those are the ways God worked to bring his Son to glory.

Why? I have no idea. But I notice one of the great ironies of life is that happiness, pursued directly, is never obtained. True happiness is a byproduct of a life of service to others and devotion to God, yet somehow even Christians feel that the pursuit of happiness is in the biblical bill of rights. But nowhere does Jesus say to pursue happiness. He says pursue him—and pick up the cross.

If your goal is to avoid suffering in life, it's a pitifully small and misguided goal, not to mention an unobtainable one. And if you try insulating yourself from pain you will also insulate yourself from the needs of people. You will become distant to those in trouble and unfeeling to suffering. You cannot become a person of true compassion unless you have walked in suffering with God.

When David's birthday party rolled around in the spring, he invited everyone. After all, he knows how it feels to be left out. So he invited the kids from his second-grade class . . . all of them including the folk from his special classes. This concerned me, since I promised to foot the bill at Lazer Tag, but deep inside I would have paid for twice as many if those who came showed love for David.

We waited at Lazer Tag for the kids to show up. We had the birthday party room reserved, the cake's candles were at attention on top of all that goopy icing, and our hearts were in our throats hoping it would be a good day for David. David seemed serenely confident.

You should have seen them pour in: fifteen children in all shapes and sizes, all colors and genders, all abilities and disabilities. Robert's mom told me that Robert had talked about nothing else for weeks. Kristin's mother said that David was the only boy in their class that was nice to her. Carl looked up at me through the thick lenses of his glasses and gave me a big hug. (Down syndrome hugs are some of the sweetest hugs I know.) Carl told David that this was the first birthday party that he had ever been invited to. And guess who else was there—the kid who teased David about repeating second grade. Big hearts keep short accounts.

They blasted each other in Lazer Tag, they sang with gusto around the birthday cake, and all the kids seemed to feel their present was the best. David thought all the presents were wonderful, and he said so. As they crowded around him to watch him open the presents, I realized that David's compassionate heart was having an impact on others. David's first eight years had some tough times, but his kind heart continues to grow, a heart that seems elusive to those who don't know hard times—maybe that's what God had in mind for David all along.

11

Sex Education and Second Chances

I *graduated* from college with a degree in microbiology. Speaking both as a microbiologist and as one who has witnessed the human birth process from start to finish three times, I would like to point out that there's much to be said for asexual budding—the reproduction method of choice for yeast. The success of spores on planet Earth is well documented, not to mention pain free. The human birth process, on the other hand, is messy and painful. It would also make things much easier for adults when it came time to explain questions about human reproduction.

"Well, son, I clipped off a bit of my fingernail, and there you were."

But God, it seems, thinks his way is best.

Like all children, ours were interested in how they were generated, and the "God gave you to us" answer lasted only till age six or so. It's the truest of answers, but it's also completely unsatisfying. Eventually they press to know the specifics of their origin.

We were driving in the car for a father-son camping trip one summer, and it became clear to me that Tristan's persistent questions needed the real story for an answer. So I nonchalantly explained the sexual processes in anatomically correct language. I was precise and frank. I made sure not to appear embarrassed or imply in any way that sex is dirty. I took pains to make it clear that sex is a gift from God.

Something else was clear: Tristan wasn't buying it. After all, it doesn't sound normal. C. S. Lewis once commented that we shouldn't knock the second birth, because the first one is strange enough. I must admit that despite my degree in biology, explaining sex was more difficult than I had expected. It must have struck Tristan that something this bizarre did not fit my cavalier manner. My words should have been delivered in the same tone and cadence as he might use when telling his friends at the lunchroom about the time when his younger brother threw up on his plate. His first questions belied his true feelings.

"Does it hurt?"

I was ready for technical questions. Still, this was one of those increasingly frequent times when Dad's fallibility was showing: sex is illogical. And Tristan, done with his technical questions, decided to play tough.

"Now, Dad," he said patronizingly, fingertips pressed together, "do you and Mom do this?" He rolled his eyes toward me for emphasis. This was not a genuine question, but a rhetorical one.

"Well, yes," I confessed.

I glanced at him. He looked stunned; he had not known me to be a liar.

"Well, Dad," he stammered, "why?!"

I smiled, and as we drove down the road I thought about that one: *Why?*

How could I describe this thing God made? The difficulty is that it's more than just making babies, and I wanted to be honest, but I became lost in thought driving down the road. An expression of love? God's expression of the oneness of Christ? I felt Tristan's earnest eyes boring into me.

Nah, he won't buy that either, I thought.

I was about to play the parental trump card: "One day you'll understand," when a vivid memory rushed to me of my dad playing the trump card with me: "One day, Mack, you'll understand." I chuckled to myself with the realization that I could pinpoint the day my dad's promise about "someday" came true: the day I met Leeann.

Love, Romance . . .

No one could have been more in love with anyone than I was with Leeann. I saw her, backlit by the rays of the setting sun streaming through the Gothic windows of . . . organic lab. Okay, so it wasn't the most romantic spot I'd ever been in, but it didn't matter. It wasn't the place (or the smell of the place), it was her. Leeann didn't walk, she floated; when she spoke I didn't hear words, I heard melodies. She didn't just smile, she lit the world with a glow of joy.

Before I met Leeann my friends thought of me as aloof and unattached, but mystically, and without explanation, they watched as I was transformed into a lover's fool. When Leeann entered pharmacy school they watched me drive seven hours from my campus to hers as if it were nothing. One sweet and tender kiss from Leeann floated me home again. I'd gone loco, my friends said. Yet they didn't know love or Leeann.

. . . and Marriage

Then we got married. We had a good honeymoon, and if our romance had been a movie it would have ended there on the promise of bliss and happiness forevermore. But we returned to a drafty apartment, my new job as a campus minister, and our own quirks and foibles that avoided destruction with the same tenacity as the roaches in our dilapidated kitchen.

Quickly we realized this marriage stuff was a lot harder than married people let on. Understanding each other's words proved tough enough. Take the vacuum cleaner I got Leeann for Valentine's Day. She's always said it's the thought that counts. She always said that she just wanted me to remember her. We needed a vacuum cleaner, and it was in nice wrapping paper. Good grief! What's all the fuss?

But there were even harder things in marriage, things that bumped against those sunken roots of our sinful nature. We began to fight, and our fights took on a disappointing sameness, scripted with slightly different words but always the same pattern: my anger and frustrations made her withdraw, making me more angry and frustrated.

It wasn't a circle as much as it was a spiral, and it looked as if we were diving downward toward the statistical pool of failed Christian marriages. Any good feeling drained out completely during the fifth year we were together. I'd like to say that a Scripture verse here and a prayer there cleared things up, but it didn't. In a way such foolish, even dangerous, thinking contributed to the problem. We had serious problems that needed to be dealt with in a serious way.

As I've reflected over those years, I've wondered how I could have been warned. What words could have been used to register the danger I was in? "Mack, I know you're in love, but you won't always feel this way." "Mack, things look rosy now, but you may go through some hard times." But even if someone had told me (and nobody did), I wouldn't have believed it. I was too much in love. Besides, calling hard times in marriage "hard times" hardly does them justice. It wasn't a hard time, it was a time of fire.

But for all our mistakes in our marriage, we finally did something right: we called for help. I remember my hand trembling when I dialed our pastor.

"Ken," I blurted after a bit of chat, "I really don't want to talk about the last elder meeting. I need to talk to you about something serious. Leeann and I are having problems, and we need some help. I don't know if we're going to make it."

Deep inside I expected Ken to drive me out of the church. But to my surprise he was not surprised: problems in marriage aren't new. Underlying the feeling that Ken would excommunicate me was the sense that God wanted to get rid of me too. I felt that God, in the words of Eugene Peterson, would tire of my fickle faith and leave me to busy himself by fulfilling prophecy in the Middle East. But I discovered that far from being done with me, God seemed to take pleasure in bringing about a rebirth of love in our marriage. We felt his care; we knew his healing. He didn't excommunicate us. He loved us into full devotion to him, and in turn to each other.

Second Chances with God

God loves giving second chances. Just think how different the Bible would be if God were a one-chance God: Abraham and Sarah's mess with their servant, Hagar, resulted in God's promise and blessing going to someone else more worthy. Abraham went back to worshiping the moon in Ur; Sarah died without bearing him an heir.

Jacob's wicked deception of his father and brother ensured

a permanent career as a shepherd in Midian.

Joseph felt sad when he learned about his father's and brothers' demise from the famine in Midian. He was tempted to feel guilty since he could have helped, but he knew ultimately the wealth he had made for himself in Egypt would serve only to enable his family's dysfunction "It's best this way," he told himself.

Moses' failed attempt at leadership that ended in murdering an Egyptian guard did little more than get his face on *Egypt's Most Wanted* weekly and launched another great career in animal husbandry in Midian.

After David topped off his unseemly love affair with murder, someone else was chosen to bear the title "Man After God's Own Heart." Bathsheba and her son were dropped from the Israelite social pages and the genealogy of Jesus.

After finding his wife, Gomer, in a strip joint, Hosea decided enough was enough. To his family's relief he settled down with a good Jewish girl when the divorce became final.

The woman caught in adultery became a biblical footnote as a proper application of the death penalty.

God zapped Saul dead on the Damascus road for killing Christians.

Thank God these are not the stories of the Bible. Thank God that the God of the Bible is a God of second chances—and third, and fourth, and seventy times seven. Still, many people don't understand. To explain this love and mercy and forgiveness to them is almost as difficult as explaining love and sex to a boy.

Joy Comes in the Morning

The pain of our marital problems are years behind us. I'm more in love with Leeann now than I ever was back in organic chemistry lab. But it took a second chance. During those times of healing in our marriage Leeann told me we were going to have a baby. Tristan's birth became a mark of regeneration in our marriage. And our children's names now remind us of God's work. Tristan means sorrow, David means beloved and Isaac means laughter. Put together they say, "Out of sorrow, beloved, there has come laughter and joy."

I contemplated all this while driving down the road, only to be interrupted by a tugging on my sleeve.

"Dad, Dad! What's wrong with your eye?"

"Huh? Oh, nothing."

"Dad, what are you thinking about?"

"Oh, I was just thinking about your mom and how much I love her."

"Dad, I'm never going to do that."

"Do what, Tristan?"

"You know, what you just told me about."

"Oh . . . right." I smiled. "Well, Tristan, one day . . . one day you'll understand."

I bet I'll even get a second chance to explain.

12

The Family Vulnerable

They called the strike at British Airways a "slow-down strike." It's a particularly maddening sort of strike: the workers go on working, but at an inefficient and sloppy pace.

"Yes, Mr. Stiles, I know you confirmed your seat reservations, and I do have you booked on the next flight to JFK, but I'm afraid there is no way that I can put these four seats together." The ticket woman had not looked at me during our entire conversation, choosing rather to stare at the computer screen.

"Please understand, Mrs. Combs," I said, reading her name off the brass nametag on her blouse, "I have a one-year-old baby, a three-year-old child, and a sick wife. We cannot sit in seats scattered around a 747." This seemed reasonable to me, but to Mrs. Combs it was only repetition.

"Please, could you stand aside, Mr. Stiles, so I might help

the man behind you?" The smile she gave me was as genuine as the question. She placed my tickets on the counter.

"Mrs. Combs, I've stood in this line for over an hour." Though my voice never rose louder than it took to be heard over jet engines, intercom announcements and the reverberations of the masses moving though the complex of Heathrow Airport, I forcefully enunciated each word: "I need something done about this."

"I'm sorry, Mr. Stiles. There's really nothing I can do." Her look, now without even the hint of a smile, would have chilled ice. She slid to her left and reached to take the other man's tickets. "Perhaps you can check again in an hour."

I walked back to Leeann, where she sat staring out the tall windows that overlooked concrete and cars. "Well, they finally have us on the flight, but our seats aren't together. They're telling me they won't change it."

She kept looking out the window. "I want to go home," she said again, softly. She seemed detached, her slender hands folded in her lap.

"I know," I said.

Tristan clung to the plastic grip of Leeann's wheelchair. He spent his time in the airport hovering wordlessly next to his mother. He intuitively understood that she was wounded and that she needed him, but he did not understand much more. David, strapped in his stroller next to Leeann's wheelchair, slept.

"Do you think it happened because we were in Africa?" Leeann asked. I looked out the window too. "No," I said.

"I just was wondering if maybe I didn't push myself too hard . . ." Her voice trailed off. She looked fatigued and a little crazy. A strand of hair strayed off on its own. Her eyes, unfocused, still turned toward the unnaturally bright British day.

I looked at my watch out of habit. "They said it may take us some extra time, because the people who are going to help you are on strike too. Our flight leaves in a couple of hours, and it's going to take every minute to get through security. It's this crazy strike."

She turned and looked up at me. "I wonder who he was?" She sounded distant, bone-weary and intensely sad.

"Me too," I said, feeling the urge to weep bubbling up in me, and wanting to, and not knowing why I didn't. We looked at each other for a moment.

"Honey, I need to get back in line. Are you going to be okay?"

Leeann nodded, then hung her head.

I did not want to be hanging around airports. I needed to get my family home. Leeann needed her mother and her home. She didn't need to be in a foreign land where everyone seemed to be on strike.

"What kind of person would have the hardheartedness to make us travel in separate seats for a six-hour flight?" I muttered to myself as I got back in line. I felt overpowering rage rising in me, rage that sprang from the feeling of powerlessness and failure. Everything seemed to be unraveling. It didn't help to be pushed around by a surly, imperial woman so drunk with her own petty power that she no longer saw people as people but only as numbers on a computer screen.

Mrs. Combs and I are going to have a little head-to-head, I thought to myself. I left thoughts of suppressing rage behind me as I moved forward in line. I prepared a speech: "Mrs. Combs, you've forgotten something: you work for me, not the other way around." I imagined rallying a revolt among the other disgruntled sheep at the ticket counter. I gritted my teeth. "KLM flies to Kenya too, you know," I grumbled to myself. I multiplied the cost of each ticket from the States to Kenya by thirty students to make sure I could quote the exact amount of our business with the airline.

The book of James says we should be slow to anger, right? I roasted mine over a slow fire and seasoned it with the spice of justice. *This might just cost her job!* I thought to myself hopefully.

The heat rose in my neck and head the closer I got to Mrs. Combs. When I finally stood face to face with her again, I wore my breastplate of righteousness readied for battle. But two things happened at once.

Mrs. Combs looked me in the eye. Just a split second; a glance, really. It was not a look of knowing—she did not remember my concerns. Hundreds fly on 747s, and on this day every one of them had a beef.

The second thing was that Tristan pulled on my pants pocket. He had ventured away from his mother's side and through the crowd to reach me.

I handed the tickets to Mrs. Combs, who took them and began typing. I knelt down to see what Tristan wanted.

"Daddy?" he asked. "Is God going to take care of us?"

To this day I don't know what prompted his question, but it was a good one. It took me aback for a second. I realized I had been wondering the same thing.

I sighed and looked down at the shiny tiled floor, then raised my eyes to Tristan. "Well, he promised he would, didn't he, Tristan?" This was more confession than teaching.

Tristan nodded.

"God will take care of us. We need to put ourselves in his hands, don't we?"

"Yes, Daddy," he said.

I rose to my full height at the counter. "Mrs. Combs," I

began. I placed my hands on the counter palm down.

"Mr. Stiles, I'm afraid there's still nothing I can do for you," Mrs. Combs said, staring at her screen.

"Mrs. Combs," I repeated louder. She looked up—she was ready for one more angry person. "I know you must have a very difficult job." She stared back with cool calm.

I don't know how to describe what happened next. Maybe it was the combination of Mrs. Combs's weary eyes and Tristan's watchful ones. Perhaps it was Tristan's question. But at any rate, I snapped. I lost it. I was nice.

"The real issue for us, Mrs. Combs, is that my wife and I just lost a little baby yesterday through a miscarriage, and we're in need of some kindness . . . just a little kindness, Mrs. Combs. Please help me." That's when I started to cry.

This was not what Mrs. Combs was expecting. Anger she understood; an emotional American male was another matter. She paused, ducked her head, then turned quickly aside. At first I thought I'd really blown it. I saw her speak to another woman behind the desk, who approached me. It was Mrs. Combs's manager, and she had my tickets in hand.

"Mr. Stiles, Mrs. Combs told me of your situation, and I can offer you four business-class tickets together and complimentary passes to the Club Lounge. Would that be okay?"

"Okay? Okay!"

Dazedly I took the new tickets and turned to go. But then I wheeled around to see Mrs. Combs looking at me sadly. "Thank you, Mrs. Combs," I said.

She nodded and said nothing, but smiled a real smile. She's a real person.

I looked down at Tristan, who was still staring up at me and hanging on my pocket, and I realized how close I'd come to another miscarriage.

A Miscarriage of Love

We tell our children the golden rule: "Treat others as you would have them treat you." When we don't practice it, it becomes a miscarriage of love, each a small death, an unrepeatable moment that could have brought bit of life. You can't have another. Oh, there may be other opportunities, just as there was another child for us, but he was not a replacement. We'll never get over our question of who was the boy we buried in London.

Once again my child had borne to me a word from the Lord: "Mack, will you believe that I will care for you, or will you take things into your own hands?"

I'll never see Mrs. Combs again. In one sense it was just a little encounter in the midst of a difficult situation. She does not remember me. The irony is that she didn't even know I did something nice. She was the one who did me a favor—I asked for kindness. She certainly didn't know what I had planned to do while standing in line. Or maybe she did?

God knew, and that's who we play to. Not to the crowd but to the coach; not to the audience but to the director. He orders our movements so that when we act according to his ways we bring life to people. We take part in what theologians call common grace: the good of God that spills over to all. Jesus phrased it like this: "You are the salt of the earth."

It's easy to see now that catching the plane was the last thing that was important. I see now that it's easy to be kind when things are going well and to act with the love of Jesus when people give us what we want. Even the pagans do that. The test comes in the hard times with difficult people. That's when it's easy to forget the Lord's care. It's frightening to be kind when things are at stake. It makes us vulnerable. It puts us in a position where others who are unscrupulous might take advantage of us. But sometimes Jesus sends us out as sheep among wolves. He asks us to give up protection and trust in his ways, to trust in him. Doing that when it made my family vulnerable was the most difficult thing I've done in life. It was also the most right.

13

Breakfast Rebuke at McDonald's

F*or the first* time in his six years of life Tristan invited me out to breakfast, and I should have wondered why. I just thought he liked breakfast out.

The night before, during our evening prayer, Tristan extended the invitation. He named the time—the next morning—and the place. The place? Only one place would meet his high standards for prompt, efficient, courteous service, where he was treated with the respect and attention due a brand-loyal customer: McDonald's.

The rising sun's cheerful rays streamed through the windows, giving a golden glow to the place. It seemed the start to a delightful morning; yet Tristan seemed oddly nervous.

As I tore the foil top off the second tub of syrup for his hotcakes, Tristan said, "Well, Dad, I guess you're wondering why I invited you for breakfast."

I chuckled at his seriousness. You might have thought he was addressing the corporate board of directors about an impromptu meeting. "Well, no, actually I just thought you liked coming to McDonald's, Tristan."

Tristan responded sternly, "Yes, I do, but I want to talk to you about something."

I stifled my grin and looked at him. His hands were folded. He rubbed the pads of his thumbs together and fidgeted.

"Okay, Tristan," I said as I cut up his hotcakes. "What do you want to tell me?"

"Dad, you know how David and I get in fights sometimes?"

"Yes, I do."

"I'm not going to do it again," he said.

"Really?"

"Yes." He paused for breath. "And I want you to know when you and Mom had that fight yesterday it scared me, and I want you not to do it again either."

You could have knocked me off that plastic chair with a Happy Meal sack.

Look how closely Tristan followed Paul's instructions in Galatians: "Brothers, if someone is caught in a sin, you who are spiritual should restore him gently. But watch yourself, or you also may be tempted. Carry each other's burdens, and in this way you will fulfill the law of Christ" (Galatians 6:1-2).

Tristan thought about my sin. He was willing to restore. He planned it out. He was gentle—he even took me out to eat. Tristan was willing to admit his own fights with his brother, and he identified with me. And he was brave enough to ask me to change.

Accountability Between Believers
The church desperately needs to hold people accountable in

this way. Christians face moral dilemmas at every level: porn on the Internet, unchecked anger in their thinking, jobs that rule the home, words that destroy, neglected marriages, neglected spiritual disciplines, habitual lying, pride and an "I don't want to be involved" attitude. Busy lives exclude many friendships, and even friendships that exist rarely hold people accountable. It's none of my business, each of us might think, or I'm not spiritual enough to point out someone else's flaws.

So it is no wonder when we see serious problems flare up from festering sin. At that point our efforts to help are usually too late and poorly executed.

When I was a young, naive campus minister, a student, Annabel, came to me and asked me to hold her accountable. Thinking accountability a good thing, I agreed.

"What is it you want me to hold you accountable for, Annabel?"

"I need to lose ten pounds."

"No problem."

Big problem! In a matter of weeks Annabel had *gained* ten pounds—and it was my fault! Why? Because in Annabel's mind, accountability for her eating patterns shifted from her to me. Her weight gain became my fault.

I don't think this is what Paul had in mind when he told us to carry each other's burdens. Rather, accountable relationships involve a series of steps that seek to restore a Christian's focus on Christ.

Gently Restore

I'm puzzled by the church's surprise at sin in their midst. What do we expect? When an American asked C. S. Lewis if God uses sinners, he responded that God has no other choice.

Don't be shocked at sin. God isn't; neither is Paul. That's why Paul prepared the Galatians with the instructions on how to deal with a fallen brother or sister. To be unprepared to deal with someone caught in sin is a prescription for disaster.

When sin rears its head in someone's life we often find it easiest to try to make it go away, usually by having the person leave. This fills the church with people who either commit sins the church accepts (gossip) or are good at hiding their sin (spousal neglect). Asking a sinner to leave drives away the honest and the snared and is the very opposite of what Paul instructs us to do.

While I believe there are situations in church discipline where we should ask people to leave the fellowship, as outlined by Jesus in Matthew 18 and by Paul in 1 Corinthians 5, our first order of business is not kicking people out of the church but doing as Paul outlines here in Galatians: to restore, gently.

Focus

Austin sat down next to me at an out-of-town convention. "Hi, Austin," I said. He was an old friend. "What's up?"

"I'm feeling strange," he said.

"Why?" I asked.

"Well, I just had a meeting with a woman our company is thinking of hiring. She seemed really interested in talking with me." Austin is a gentle, thoughtful person, and lots of people like talking to him.

"Well, Austin, what's so strange about that? Lots of people want to talk with you."

"I don't know."

"Really, Austin, what do you mean?"

"I guess what's strange is I really liked talking with her."

"Austin, this is very serious," I said. I probed some more, and I told him I appreciated his telling me. I shared with him failures I'd witnessed. Then I risked by sharing with him deeply my own struggles with sexual sin and the safeguards I've found helpful. It felt as if I were stepping off a high dive and didn't know how to swim. It's scary to share vulnerably with others about our sin—but it's worth it.

Austin at first acted as if I had gone overboard. Maybe he was shocked about how sinful I was! But a situation such as this needs to be taken seriously.

"Nothing's happened," he protested.

I said, "First, that's the best time to take care of it, when nothing's happened, and second, something did happen: you felt strange, and that's enough."

Lately I've decided it's better to go overboard and be wrong than to risk one more ship's getting grounded on the reef. Temptations are worth being wrong about, but when they run unchecked they cause shipwrecks. And when one person responds, it's worth it.

I checked with Austin over the course of that year by phone and touched base at meetings. I made it a point to ask about his marriage and if his feelings were in check. Two years later we were at another conference, and Austin called my room. "Can I speak with you down in the lobby?" he asked.

"Sure," I said.

We sat in the lobby on the plastic couch by the coatroom. "Mack, I just wanted to take a minute to thank you for saving my life." Austin then went on to tell me how with hindsight he now sees what danger he was in. He said he especially appreciated my vulnerability regarding my own sin.

Believe me, it was worth it for that. Just a gentle nudge that brings focus is often all that's needed.

Watch Yourself

It takes vulnerability to ask personal questions. It also takes an examined life. Paul's call for an examined life comes because he knows we cannot restore others with integrity unless we are dealing with our own sin. You don't have to have a perfect life, but just a willingness to do what you ask others to do. Part of the examined life is to give and to seek permission for accountability structures.

"William, you're on the Internet all the time," I said. "Do you even feel tempted by pornography?"

I heard William pause and inhale. I pressed the phone to my ear.

"Mack, I've got to tell someone," he said. "It's become a real snare to me."

Only months before my friend Brian and I started to surf the Net at about the same time, and we made a commitment to each other to avoid all pornography on the Net. I wasn't worried about this being a problem, but I know my own capacity for sin too, so we checked with each other occasionally.

But as I helped hold William accountable, the ins and outs of pornography on the Internet became more obvious. As he told me how he had become caught, I found myself wondering what it would be like. Just curious, you know? It couldn't hurt anyone . . . no one would ever know. . . . The danger of Internet pornography is its anonymity. I'm convinced that if I did not have the commitment to Brian I could have very easily have been snared by the web of pornography on the Internet too. It convinced me of the wisdom of Paul's instructions: guard yourself. See to it you don't stumble either.

Accountability Means Carrying Burdens

An unwillingness to carry burdens is odious to God. When we

deal with restoring the fallen by definition we're dealing with sin, so we must ready ourselves to carry some burdens.

In Galatians Paul says that to carry burdens fulfills the law of Christ. This is in sharp contrast to the law of Moses. The law of Christ, unlike the Mosaic law, involved serving others, washing other people's feet. What a wonderful way to fulfill the law.

I'm still helping William. William is convinced that his wife needs to know of his addiction, but how will she respond? I don't know. There may be pieces to pick up, and I'm going to be there for him.

When Tristan and I got home from our breakfast at McDonald's, I took Leeann by the hand. "Honey, I have something very important to tell you." Tristan watched from the doorway. Leeann's left eyebrow went up, and she turned her head a bit. She had half a smile on her face.

"You remember our fight yesterday, don't you?" Now the other eyebrow went up in surprise.

"Just stay with me, dear," I whispered.

"Why yes, now that you mention it, I do," she said.

"Well, I want to ask your forgiveness and tell you that to the best of my ability I'll not do it again."

"Okay." No longer able to contain herself, she asked, "What did you and Tristan talk about at McDonald's?"

"Never mind. I just want to know if you forgive me."

"Yes."

We hugged. "I love you very much."

Tristan smiled and turned to go outside. I stopped him and said, "Tristan, thanks for breakfast—and for being brave."

"You're welcome, Dad," he said.

The door slammed. Leeann turned and said, "What in the world is going on?"

Now, neither Leeann nor I could remember details of the argument, and though I'm sure it's true that Leeann and I argued about something, it didn't register with us. We marveled at children's sensitivity and wondered if there would be more strength in the church if we took each other so thoughtfully—and biblically. And it wasn't all that bad for our relationship, either.

In fact, after Tristan and my conversation at McDonald's, Leeann and I took time to examine our words to each other. We agreed it can't hurt to speak with more love. And though we've had some arguments since then, we explained to Tristan our commitment to fair fighting. We'll fight, but in a civil tone, while avoiding "cheap shots." We've found eating and arguing at nice restaurants helpful in keeping this commitment—another thing I've learned from my kids. And we get to go to nicer restaurants than McDonald's.

14

Plastic Hammers
Can Do
Lots of Damage

The rewiring of the VCR to my old stereo system turned out to be a bigger project than I had foreseen. Trying to get the right plug in the right socket though a sea of wiring so consumed my attention that the faint sounds of hammering registered only faintly. Then Isaac appeared at the foot of the stairs.

"Um . . . hey, Dad," said Isaac with feigned nonchalance.

"Hi, Isaac," I said, holding the red right speaker cord while wondering if the yellow socket on the amplifier that said "right play" was input or output.

"Dad, um, whatcha doing?"

"I'm trying to make our speakers work."

"Oh," he said. Usually after this question Isaac is off and running, but that day he stood rooted to the stair.

"Uh, Dad . . . ?"

"Yes, Isaac?"

"Dad?"

"What, Isaac?" I said, finally looking up from my mess.

It was then I noticed he was directing his gaze toward his shoes. "Did you . . . hear something a little while ago?" he asked.

"No. Well, maybe . . . Why? What's up, Isaac?"

"Dad," he asked, "how much does a wall cost?"

"A lot, Isaac. Why?"

Isaac's eyes grew large and watery. I began to wonder what his bedroom wall looked like. A four-year-old and a hammer can do a lot of damage.

"Um, Dad . . . ," his voice squeaked. "Dad, you know that picture I drew that you really liked?"

"Your self-portrait from preschool. Yeah."

"Well, I just wanted to put it in a place where you could see it all the time and . . ." At this point, unable to continue this rehearsed speech, he burst into tears and a jumble of words.

"Daddy, I'm really sorry. Really, I am. Oh, I didn't mean to hurt the wall . . . I didn't know how to put it up and I just wanted to, to . . ."

What concern I had for the wall melted with this tortured confession. "Whoa there, big guy," I said, stumbling over my wires to get to him. I put my arm around him.

"Wait, slow down," I said as I put him on my knee. He gasped for air in between his sobs.

"Listen, you know how much effort and money Mom and Dad have put into this house, don't you?"

"Y-y-yeah," he wailed.

"But you know what?"

"What?" he said, hiccuping for air.

"Compared to our love for you, this house doesn't mean anything."

"Really?" he said with genuine surprise.

"That's right," I said. "In fact, Isaac, there's not a thing that I own that I wouldn't gladly give up for you, including this house."

"Hmmm," said Isaac. His eyes narrowed. "What about your computer?"

"Isaac, I love you more than my computer."

"Hmmm," he said, mulling this over.

"It's true Isaac. Now give me a hug, and let's go see the shape of your wall."

He took me by the hand and showed me where he had hung his picture. If he had not confessed, we might not have even noticed. He had taken a straight pin and carefully tacked the picture to the wall, where it stayed for months. The plastic hammer had made some red marks and small dents on the wall, but it wasn't anything to worry about. That is, unless you're four, and you think you've done something very bad, and you're not sure how to find forgiveness.

More Than Just Forgiving Ourselves

I'm fascinated by how strikingly unhelpful psychotherapy was in dealing with guilt during the last century. Freud truly wanted to heal people (something that he grew increasing cynical about over the years), and to this end Freud's focus of therapy dealt with behavior. The goal was to help people avoid destructive behavior in the future. The problem with this, obviously, is that there's not much to be done with feelings of guilt. They were, after all, feelings about things in the past. So if a heinous sin existed in someone's life, the most a therapist could say was "Move on with your life" or "You need to forgive yourself." That's why the highest goals in most psychotherapy is self-acceptance or a good self-image, regardless of our true image.

A good self-image is not a bad thing; it's just that it has serious limits as an ultimate life goal. It doesn't deal with our fervent need to live in forgiveness for past wrongs. Deep inside we long for more than just forgiving ourselves—we desire the forgiveness of God.

I use a media program with university students to see how Hollywood deals with biblical issues. It's called "Jesus and the Media." In our curriculum we use a clip from Steven Spielberg's film *Schindler's List* to underscore the weakness of self-forgiveness.

The movie tells the true story of Oskar Schindler, a German man who during World War II used Jewish slave labor to run his factory and save their lives. The clip starts with a scene of mass panic in the concentration camp. The commandant is on the balcony of his mansion overlooking the camp, methodically shooting Jewish slave workers who appear idle. The panic of the camp comes in waves, orchestrated by the movement and direction of his high-powered hunting rifle.

A following scene is of a wild party that evening at the commandant's mansion. Champagne spews while the drunk commandant grabs and forcibly kisses beautiful women. After the party the commandant is alone with his friend, Schindler, on the same balcony where he randomly shot innocent people only hours earlier. The balcony is backlit with the glare of prison searchlights.

Though Schindler's factory makes war materials, his subtle agenda is to use his influence to prevent the executions of Jews. Perhaps the previous day's shooting is on Schindler's mind as they discuss power. The commandant tells Schindler the Jews fear the Nazis because they have the power to kill them. Schindler disagrees: "Power is when we have every justification to kill and we don't."

"You think that's power?" retorts the commandant.

"That's what the emperor said. A man stole something, he's brought in to the emperor, he throws himself down on the ground, he begs for mercy—he knows he's going to die, and the emperor pardons him. He's a worthless man—he lets him go."

"I think you are drunk."

Schindler points to the commandant. "That's power, Amond. That is power." He pauses, smiles, then points to the commandant. "Amond the good!"

At this the commandant snorts, mockingly points back to Schindler and with an inebriated laugh says, "I pardon you."

But the commandant only appeared to dismiss Schindler's philosophy. The next day he goes about his business offering pardon for trespasses that previously would have merited death: a Jewish worker drops the commandant's expensive saddle, and he forgives him. A Jewish woman is caught smoking on the job, and he pardons her. The Jewish boy who scrubs his bathtub is unable to remove the stain, and after the commandant shows the boy how to correctly clean the stain he dismisses him, saying: "Go, I pardon you."

The boy leaves, making his way back to the concentration camp across the long yard that spreads out under the ominous balcony. At the boy's departure the commandant turns to see himself in the bathroom mirror. He brushes aside his forelock and points to himself. His bent, limp fingers slowly touch the mirror, forming an ironic anti-image: that of Michelangelo's *Creation of Man* from the Sistine Chapel. Then the commandant, as if repeating his words to the boy, says to himself, "I pardon you."

But the fingers belong to a guilty man and his own image, not a new creation touched by God, created in God's image, filled with new life. He's powerless to remove the stain of his sin, powerless to give himself new life. His only power is destroying. In his desire to become good and give pardon it becomes clear he is the one who most needs pardon and so faces the futility and pointlessness, even silliness, of self-forgiveness.

This brief moment of self-study passes as the commandant notices his fingernails and examines them with interest. He then picks up his rifle and shoots the young boy before he reaches the outside gate of the camp.

Real Forgiveness

Spielberg's troubling image accents the futility of pardoning oneself. Who could tell the commandant to "forgive himself" and "move on"? Helping someone with self-image problems while ignoring their guilt is like cleaning their fingernails while there is blood on their hands.

Jesus told people the good news was that God forgives sin freely, lavishly for all who ask. Jesus told it this way:

There was a man who had two sons. The younger one said to his father, "Father, give me my share of the estate." So he divided his property between them.

Not long after that, the younger son got together all he had, set off for a distant country and there squandered his wealth in wild living. After he had spent everything, there was a severe famine in that whole country, and he began to be in need. So he went and hired himself out to a citizen of that country, who sent him to his fields to feed pigs. He longed to fill his stomach with the pods that the pigs were eating, but no one gave him anything.

When he came to his senses, he said, "How many of my father's hired men have food to spare, and here I am starving to death! I will set out and go back to my father and say to him: Father, I have sinned against heaven and against you. I am no longer worthy to be called your son; make me like one of your hired men." So he got up and went to his father.

But while he was still a long way off, his father saw him and was filled with compassion for him; he ran to his son, threw his arms around him and kissed him.

The son said to him, "Father, I have sinned against heaven and against you. I am no longer worthy to be called your son."

But the father said to his servants, "Quick! Bring the best robe and put it on him. Put a ring on his finger and sandals on his feet. Bring the fattened calf and kill it. Let's have a feast and celebrate. For this son of mine was dead and is alive again; he was lost and is found." So they began to celebrate. (Luke 15:11-24)

There are subtleties in this story that are missed today. For instance, the younger son's wish for his inheritance implied a wish for his father's death. It was as if he had said: "I wish you were dead so I could have your money." The boy had broken the fifth commandment, which dealt with honoring fathers and mothers (Exodus 20:12). Insolence and disobedience of this sort merited not only the father's judgment, but also judgment by the entire community. But the surprise to those who heard Jesus tell this story is that the father gave him the money.

And as Jesus tells this story it becomes clear this young man could sink no lower: a father hater and a fool who squanders a fortune only to serve foreigners by fattening their pigs. He is not just feeding pigs, the most unclean of the unclean animals, but wanting to eat what they ate. This brought the same revulsion to Jewish people of Jesus' day as we might feel toward the commandant of a concentration camp.

But he comes to his senses. "I'll hire myself out," he says. He memorizes a speech to tell his dad, a job offer, as it were, and heads home.

The second surprise to those listening is that the father has been watching. The father, not the son, is the one who rushes to greet him. Older, successful men in Middle Eastern culture don't run—their robes and their pride don't allow it, but this father picks up his robes, humiliating himself, and runs to his son. The boy begins his speech, but it's unimportant, for he has grossly underestimated the lavish love and forgiveness of his father.

"Quick," says the father. "Let's have a party!" When we look in the mirror and really see ourselves for who we are, we must turn to the Father rather than to ourselves if we are to know true forgiveness of sin. Just a childlike confession, as simple and humble as Isaac's confession to me.

Isaac's instinctive desire for pardon mimics our own. We need pardon from God, not from ourselves, for the waywardness that gnaws at our hearts, waywardness as quaint as Isaac's dents on a bedroom wall and as serious as murder. And just like Isaac, our humble confessions melt the heart of our heavenly Father. I took Isaac very seriously. I told him that I forgave him and loved him. I said, "Isaac, never forget that God is a loving Father, and that you can always turn to him when you do wrong." I hope he always remembers. I hope I never forget.

15

Teaching Dad
How to Play

It *is obvious to* children, but largely unknown to adults, that few grownups remember how to play.

There are delightful exceptions. My mother is often found under the dining-room table with David or Isaac, playing the part of pirate prisoner. She plays this role so well that it almost seems as if her stiff joints come from the dankness of the pirate hangout, not because of her sixty-seven-year-old knees. But she is an elite in the grownup population. Most of us must have children reteach what we have forgotten.

David, Isaac and I were playing a typical mixed-metaphor game: dinosaurs and Beanie Babies party together, taking spins on the remote-controlled truck before being attacked by Lego men riding stomp rockets. We were in their room on the floor surrounded by the odd conglomeration of boxes, plastic and Lego parts.

In this particular round of make-believe I was given charge of the green-and-white cloth cow. The cow's head was sewn on in such a way that it flopped back and forth. It's an entry-level toy. Isaac and David took the higher-level dinosaurs.

"What's the feeding schedule for this cow?" I asked. I started making mooing noises. I was really pleased with both my sound effects and the motions I was making with the cow's legs.

"Has it been milked today?" I wondered out loud. "Let's build a Lego fence so this cow can have some pasture." It took me a few minutes to realize that David was not playing anymore. He was watching.

I assumed it was that my cowlike moaning, my stunning play, that so caught their attention. I knew they were happy to sit back and just enjoy my playful antics. But as Isaac stared and David alternately looked at me then up at the ceiling, it became clear something was wrong.

David finally interrupted by placing his hand on my arm and fixing his gaze on me. He pondered how to tell me something rather difficult.

"Dad." His tone said he didn't want to hurt my feelings.

I stopped force-feeding my green-and-white cow.

"Dad," he said again, "it's not a real animal, you know." Isaac nodded his agreement.

My play seemed too serious, I guess. I'd unknowingly moved from "play" and celebrating to the grownup world of striving. David saw it happen and wanted to help. What mysterious line I had crossed was as clear to David as it was cloudy to me. I just didn't have it.

Competition

I know I'm not there because I still scarcely know what to call the opposite of play—that line between fun and competition, between play and prize, between frolic and march, between party and tournament, so understood by children, so missed by adults.

I see it most often when I'm an assistant coach for my son's soccer team. Adults' desire to win a prize tends to ruin the game for kids. Understand, though, that I'm for competition.

Competition gives games a point. It's the "hope" part of sport. Competition helps us persevere even if we're no good when we start. Competition develops discipline and the building of character. It keeps our eyes on the prize; it helps us see delayed gratification as a good thing. Competition transforms little girls playing ballet to actually performing on the stage, it keeps three-foot Isaac heaving basketballs to an eight-foot vertical height even though the hoop is ten feet off the ground.

Yet competition devoid of play becomes tyrannical and ugly: the ends justify the means, and winning a prize becomes everything. Without play in our games we do very strange things. One parent really told me, "I want you to teach my child to play to win." Or we do even crazier things like turning basketball players into zillionaires. Admittedly, they play basketball very well, but it's just basketball, and those guys aren't having fun, they're just doing a job. All that is left for them is a prize; play is gone.

That's why we must have a sense that play is a part of sport, or ballet, or life. The competitive beast is held at bay by play, by frolicking and celebrating play. In a competitive world there's no point to frolicking. You don't win if you frolic. Young lovers frolic, children frolic, but it's hard to imagine pro football players frolicking.

The good things in a sense of play are enjoyment, fellowship, understanding the big picture, developing a love of the game, merriment and discovery. I admit that play devoid of competition or striving can give a pointlessness to being, but ultimately so does unbridled competition—we just get there later rather than sooner.

There's need for a sense of play outside sports; play is needed in many things in life. Academics, for example. Who is the real lover of literature: our small group, sitting in the living room discussing the book we've read, or David upstairs reading *Charlotte's Web* under the bedcovers? David is. The grownups have forgotten why they read or how to enter into another world. The grownups have forgotten how to lose themselves in play. (See C. S. Lewis's *An Experiment in Criticism* [1992 edition, Cambridge University Press].)

Play in Our Spiritual Lives

Without play our prayers become lists to check off rather than times of enjoying the presence of the Lord. Without play the best reader of his Bible study notes wins. Without play worship becomes a performance. Without play it's hard to rejoice in Christ when good ministry is done—by other ministries. Spiritual disciplines become scientific and mechanical, and we lose interest in the journey, asking only, "When are we going to get there?" Without play we can't love—after all, love, like play, is pointless.

Without play we become the older brother of the prodigal son who won't come in to the party.

The older brother became angry and refused to go in. So his father went out and pleaded with him. But he answered his father, "Look! All these years I've been slaving for you and never disobeyed your orders. Yet you never gave me even a young goat so I could celebrate with my friends. But when this son of yours who has squandered your property with prostitutes comes home, you kill the fattened calf for him!"

"My son," the father said, "you are always with me, and everything I have is yours. But we had to celebrate and be glad, because this brother of yours was dead and is alive again; he was lost and is found." (Luke 15:28-32)

What's amazing about the older brother, despite his view of himself, is he's every bit the sinner his younger brother is. He shames his father by throwing a temper tantrum during a joyful celebration. He humiliates his father by requiring his father to leave the party to beg and plead. His list of self-righteous complaints slanders his father: he calls him a task master. He claims his father is a miser since he feels that the father has given him nothing (though it's clear in the story that the father has divided his wealth between his sons). His blinding anger stems from a competitive nature: he compares how little his father has given him and how much he's given his worthless brother.

His party with a goat would be to celebrate with his friends, not with his dad. Anyway, he even refuses to acknowledge his brother as his brother, calling him "this son of yours." So intent is he to slander his brother, calling him a whoremonger—though Jesus makes it clear he lost his money only in lavish living—that it blinds him to his father's joy and celebration of new life.

But the worst of it is that it blinds him to his own need. Those who enter the party find life, those who don't find death. Unlike his brother, he has not come to his senses; he refuses to enjoy his father's love and acceptance. His intent is to win, but he's forgotten how to play.

Celebration and Play

That's the good news of Jesus: all who come to their senses

are welcome to the party—older and younger brothers. Pardon is freely given at the Father's party. But we must be willing to play, not compete with each other.

So celebrate. Go to the party. Play puts enjoyment into spiritual disciplines as we enjoy the presence of God. Play helps us love discovery in the Christian journey and helps us hope for what is to come. Play frees us to see the big picture so we're shooting lions in the spiritual battle, not mice. Play keeps our competitive nature in check so we're not so worried what this brother got or what that sister did, but instead we celebrate, frolic, love as the family of God.

If you don't have kids, borrow some, and let them teach you how to play. I'd loan you my mom, but she's downstairs under the table with her grandkids.

Light

You are the light
of the world.
MATTHEW 5:14

16

Bedtime Stories

B*edtime is* an absolute in our family. Nobody, *nobody,* gets to stay up past their bedtime. Not ever.

Leeann convinced me that rigid rules work best with children at bedtime. She read a book about being consistent with children at bedtimes. The book proposed a simple theory: infants learn to get what they want by crying, but if they're fed and warm and dry but still cry it's no longer a request for a need, but a manipulation. Leeann's book acknowledged that it's hard to tow the line with your kids at bedtime, especially crying infants, but you must. It's for their own good. When bedtime rules are ignored, the family starts down the slippery slope from simple nighttime purgatory to heaven knows what kind of broken rules. It made sense to me, so I enforced bedtime rules vigilantly.

It was only later I came to realize Leeann's views on bedtime had nothing to do with the book. Her views rested in her love of sleep, and if the children didn't sleep well, neither did we. (She would say neither did *she,* since I tend to sleep through anything.) I've wondered at times if Leeann didn't make up the bumper sticker that says, "Consciousness: that annoying time between naps."

Looking back, I'm convinced that Leeann's protection of her sleep is what made it easy to get our kids to bed with such ease. But our children are trained. In the meantime our family joke has become "Sometimes I wake up grumpy; other times I let her sleep."

I was speaking at the men's retreat for Asbury College. Tristan had come too. It was late and nearing his bedtime, but as we headed for our room, Nate, an earnest freshman, approached me. "Would you mind talking with my roommate? He's seeking God, and I've told him all I know."

I smiled as I wondered how long that took. "Sure. I'd love to talk with him." Then I hesitated, thinking about Tristan's bedtime. Leeann had made me promise that if Tristan went with me I would make sure he got to bed on time.

Nate continued, "He's from Sweden, and he didn't know Asbury was a Christian college, so it's really been . . . um . . . interesting."

"Okay," I said, to Tristan's delight. "You don't think he'd mind if Tristan came, do you?"

Andreas, tall, blond and reserved, told me he had chosen Asbury because it seemed to be in an interesting part of the country, and he'd wanted to get out of Sweden for a while.

And Asbury sure is Christian. When Andreas arrived, he discovered Nate had plastered one wall of his dorm room with a flag of a cross, his professors actually professed Christianity, and the woman he asked out for a date was "a lot of fun—but," Andreas said, "she was different, because . . ." He struggled for the right English word. "She's a very committed Christian. I mean, she really takes this stuff *seriously!* There's a lot of rules here."

Small wonder Andreas has questions about Christianity, I thought to myself. It was to become an opportunity I'm glad I didn't miss. I'm glad I broke the rules. Tristan was going to see something much better than following the rules.

The Rules

Sometimes I worry about the rules of dealing with people outside the faith. Much of it just seems like manipulation. And I'm disgusted with much of modern-day evangelism in America; at least with much of what is pawned off as evangelism. It's a thinly disguised imitation for the gospel.

I find three deadly unwritten rules about dealing with outsiders:

1. Answer all the questions non-Christian ask with the skill of a Ph.D. in apologetics.

2. Don't say anything that may offend.

3. Make sure you get people to pray a prayer of salvation, even if you resort to trickery.

But Paul said, "Be wise in the way you act toward outsiders; make the most of every opportunity. Let your conversation be always full of grace, seasoned with salt, so that you may know how to answer everyone" (Colossians 4:5-6).

Breaking Rule 1: Avoid Useless Apologetics

Paul said to be wise in your dealing with non-Christians. Paul did not say be knowledgeable with outsiders, but wise! To miss wisdom is to become as wise as doves and as harmless as serpents. It's no wonder many Christians shy away from giving a defense for their faith: the model often championed is to overwhelm the opposition with an abrasive spirit and a Ph.D. Shed the desire to prove Jesus; you can't, any more than you can prove Caesar or Churchill. (No more than they can *disprove* Jesus, or Caesar or Churchill, for that matter.) Tell people you understand the message comes with wild claims. But if it's from God, wouldn't we expect it to?

Many people want a list of rules for how to act with outsiders. They want a list of exactly when to do things. But bedtimes, evangelism and life in general do not work that way. This is as close as it comes: ask questions, then listen to people. The great temptation after you have memorized the answers to "What about all those hypocrites in the church?" "What happens to the people who have never heard?" or "Why is the Bible authoritative?" is to blurt out the answers before you find the real issue. But if you haven't listened to their words and heart you are in danger of missing the real issues. Besides, it can be a real waste of time to spend useless hours talking theological points that serve only to screen a person from dealing with the claims of Jesus.

After exchanging some pleasantries, Andreas began his inquiry of the Christian faith with the zeal of a prosecuting attorney. "First, I don't really understand the blood atonement of Jesus. Why was he required to be crucified? Propitiation, I think it's called."

I swallowed. *Good grief, this is first?* I thought and repented of thinking that Nate didn't know much about the faith.

My mind began to whirl. If I could just remember the distinction between propitiation and expatiation . . . I wondered if perhaps the best place to start was Genesis: how the brokenness of Adam and Eve brought death and the hint of sacrifice as God brought animal skins for them to wear. Perhaps

I needed to outline the series of blood sacrifices God required in the Old Testament law. I could talk about Passover and its amazing parallel with the sacrifice of Jesus. Maybe I needed to help Andreas understand the depth of our sin and the need of Christ's work on the cross . . .

Actually, no. None of the above. Is propitiation important? You bet it is. Could I answer a question about propitiation? Yes, in a variety of ways. Was it the conversation that I needed to be having with Andreas at the time? Not at all.

"Andreas," I said, "it's a complex issue. I'm not sure I even understand all the ins and outs, but are you sure this is the thing that bothers you about Christianity?"

"Yes," he said, but then his faced furrowed, and he grabbed the front of his metal folding chair. "Well, I am puzzled about that, but no, that's not what's bothering me, not really."

"Well, Andreas, what is?"

Andreas said quietly, "What's really on my heart is that I sense God is after me, and I feel frightened."

I'm glad I asked! Not only did I avoid a potentially empty theological discussion, but I talked with Andreas about his heart. That's what I was looking for. I suspect that's what you're looking for in discussions with nonbelievers too.

Notice what helped us talk about something real was a question, not an answer. Think how I might have missed a very important discussion with Andreas if wisdom hadn't prevailed over my knowledge.

Breaking Rule 2: Don't Manipulate

It's after Paul's counsel to be wise that he coaches us to talk. (Many Christians get that order wrong too.) He says we should let our "conversation be always full of grace, seasoned with salt."

We're to have conversation—not monologue. And it should be full of grace and seasoned with salt. I take that to mean we should speak with people in ways that reflect the mercy and grace we have been given by God, but not neglect truth. Correct nonbiblical ideas if they are critical to a person's understanding of the gospel. It's true that no one has ever been argued into the kingdom, but an unanswered question or misinformed prejudice can prevent someone from coming to Christ. Sweep them away with gentle, thoughtful answers.

Leave other big issues alone if they don't have something to do with a person's understanding of Jesus: politics, homosexuality, abortion and the like. At the same time, avoid the temptation to sugarcoat ideas that are not biblical. (Paul said salt, not sugar.) When I figured out what issue most concerned Andreas, I felt free to correct hindrances to the gospel. Here's how I seasoned my conversation with Andreas with salt.

"Andreas," I continued, "you know it's a dangerous thing to be pursued by God."

"Why?" Andreas crossed his arms. He fully expected me to tell him he was going to hell.

"He may stop," I said.

This caught Andreas a bit off guard, but after a few seconds he said, "No, I have read that he won't. It's in the book of Romans."

"Oh, yes, Andreas, I know that passage. It's one of my favorites: 'Nothing will separate us from the love of Christ.' But you see, Andreas, that's for Christians, those who were called by God and are now in a relationship with him. Not you."

"Oh," he said.

I did not say this with glee. I was impressed that he was reading the Bible. (Nate was also becoming more impressive to me.) I was torn with the deep desire, the temptation, to comfort a young man who was frightened, honest and noble. But it would have been sinister. Many, in their desire to create goodwill, crucify the truth.

As Andreas thought about this I said, "Andreas, when you decide to follow Jesus you will have a stronger faith because you've thought through these issues."

"Well," he said, "I've been told if I decide to follow Jesus he will meet my needs and my life will get very good."

This seemed to Andreas to be a point in Christianity's favor. But I faced another temptation: to make it sound better than it is.

"No, Andreas. No!" I said.

Andreas blinked his surprise.

"Actually, Andreas, you may accept Jesus and find that life goes very badly for you."

"What do you mean?" he asked.

"Well, you may find that your friends reject you, you could lose your job, your family might oppose your decision—there's a host of bad things that may happen to you if you decide to follow Jesus. Andreas, when Jesus calls you he calls you to go the way of the cross."

Andreas stared back and asked the obvious: "Then why would I want to follow Jesus?"

Sadly, this is the question that stumps many Christians. For some reason we feel that unless we're meeting people's needs they won't follow Christ. Yet this is not the gospel.

I cocked my head. "Because Jesus is true. This stuff really happened."

Break the rules. Don't be afraid of the truth; it's very powerful. Some will be offended, but if people are genuinely interested and we express concern and credibility, they will listen to some hard, salty things.

Breaking Rule 3: Allow the Spirit to Work

The conversation ebbed. Andreas said he wasn't quite ready to give his life to Christ.

This is big. The rules say press for a decision. The rules say he might die in a car wreck and his blood will be on my hands. The rules say that the last thing I want right before I enter the pearly gates is Andreas glaring at me as he gets on the bus to hell, mouthing to me, "You should have done better."

But I actually agreed with him. I believe the sovereignty of God is more important than my technique. "It's a big decision, and you should think it through," I said.

Andreas took a walk to do that. And though the hour was late, I took Nate and Tristan outside under a canopy of stars to pray. Tristan, who had listened to the whole conversation with wide-eyed attention, prayed a heartfelt prayer for Andreas to come to know the Lord. We set up a time for Nate and Andreas to come out to our house for dinner and meet the rest of the family in about two weeks.

But before our dinner date arrived, Andreas decided to follow Christ. Nate called with the news. He sounded happy about the decision Andreas had made but rather glum that the one who had actually prayed a prayer of commitment with Andreas was the girl Andreas had asked out for a date. I thought that was pretty funny, and a lot like God.

Our dinner together was a celebration of Andreas's new life in Christ. Andreas told us the whole story. It encouraged all of us—especially Tristan. Andreas told us he wanted to tell someone the good news, so he conversed with his best friend in Sweden over the Internet. "Yeah, he gave his life to Jesus too," he said.

I suspended my fork midway between mouth and peas. "Andreas, you led your best friend to Christ over the Internet?"

"Yeah. The Internet is amazing, isn't it?" he said.

"Well, yes, it is . . . but Andreas, you led your friend to Christ?" I repeated dumbly.

"Yeah," he said as he scooped his third helping of roast beef onto his plate. "Jesus is pretty exciting, and I've been thinking about it a lot lately, and I've got a lot to tell."

Andreas had other things to tell, or more accurately, ask. He asked the girl who led him to the Lord to marry him, and she agreed. The wedding was fun—even Tristan enjoyed it. Well, he was glad he got a piece of cake. The rest he could have missed, especially the kissy part. Leeann cried at the wedding as she always does. We let the kid stay up late. After all, sometimes the rules are made to be broken.

17

What Page
Are You On?

O*ne summer* we made our home in Tunisia, North Africa. The fifteen American students we brought with us lived in Muslim homes. The housing situations for the students were rewarding but intense, so they often visited our apartment on the weekends for fellowship and anything resembling American food. During one Sunday spaghetti lunch I began an innocent conversation with our middle son, David. At least it began innocently.

A number of years before I had made a naive decision to answer all my children's "why" questions. I thought it would be fun. But that was before they talked. So when David turned four he began asking "why" with the zeal of a researcher bent on winning the Nobel Prize.

"David, please stop messing with your noodles and eat your spaghetti."

"Why?" he asked. He looked so nonchalant, so innocent, but he was drawing me in.

"Well, because Mom made spaghetti for you to eat."

"Why?"

"Well, because you like spaghetti."

"Why?" Suddenly, without notice, we were on the topic of cultural anthropology.

"David, you like spaghetti because people from different cultures have different tastes and likes, and you happen to like spaghetti."

My answers were coming a bit slower, but David's question hadn't changed its monosyllabic simplicity or speed. "Why?"

A philosophical question on free will, I thought as I rubbed my chin. "Well . . ." I stumbled, "it's a function of freedom to choose what we want in life, in nonmoral issues."

David smiled at me sweetly. He had me right where he wanted me: thoughts of his finishing his noodles had long left my mind.

The students found this interchange delightful too. I, on the other hand, realized that we have a choice in both nonmoral and moral issues, but wondered if I wanted to mention this correction to my four-year-old, or worse, the college students. Notice that it doesn't take many "whys" to get to the end of a thorny question.

I was just about to play my trump card—"Because I told you so"—when David asked, "Why?"

David had succeeded in taking noodles to an unprecedented level of theological debate. *Augustine lived not ten miles from here,* I thought to myself. *Maybe this is how he got his start.* At least theology was an area I felt some competence. "David," I said triumphantly, "you can eat your noodles because you're free—you're free in Christ!"

But as I raised my hands in the air to punctuate my point. David dropped his head and stared at his plate. He looked crushed. He slowly shook his head and whispered in a defeated voice, "Daddy . . . I'm not free."

The students dropped their cheerful banter and stared at David. His lower lip trembled. Leeann passed the Parmesan cheese and a concerned glance. David had always been our thoughtful and sensitive child; what insight did his young mind carry about spiritual freedom? What bondage could a four-year-old know in his heart?

While we pondered his possible thoughts, David seemed to gain some kind of inner grit. As he gazed at the plate, his knuckles went white, gripping his Sesame Street fork. I could see something click deep in his mind. His brown eyes blazed. As he prepared to speak, he wiped his mouth, smearing spaghetti sauce across both cheeks. He clutched both sides of his seat and raised himself to the full height of the Tunisian phone book. "Daddy," he announced, exhaling each word with righteous indignation, "I'm not free. *I'm four!*"

It was then, we realized, that I had come close to a four-year-old's unpardonable sin. I had accused him of being three—in Christ. We weren't on the same page.

On Different Pages

The author of the book of Hebrews knew how it felt. In the first five chapters of his book he gives his group of youngsters in Christ a quick summary Christ's position in heaven and on earth. Then he carefully outlines a tight case for Jesus as high priest in the order of Melchizedek. Admittedly this discussion was theological gristle, but the point was significant and worth chewing on.

By chapter 5 the author decides his audience wasn't on the

same page. Perhaps an angry memory triggered the writer to digress—a memory perhaps of a deacon asleep on the front row, the earnest mom merely wondering if she'd turned off the coffeemaker, the dull student lifting his hand to ask, "Is this going to be on the test?"

Whatever the reason for his anger, it's as if he has put down the pen and set his hands on his hips to lecture: "We have much to say about this, but it is hard to explain because you are slow to learn." Sometimes translations make the biblical language more dignified than it really is. What he is really saying is "I've had it with your spiritual immaturity."

And he doesn't stop there. "In fact, though by this time you ought to be teachers, you need someone to teach you the elementary truths of God's word all over again. You need milk, not solid food!" And while he is giving his flock the spiritual "what for," he gives us a marvelous definition of spiritual maturity. This admonition on spiritual maturity is a biblical oddity. It's rare that Scripture talks about spiritual maturity in such a direct way.

> Anyone who lives on milk, being still an infant, is not acquainted with the teaching about righteousness. But solid food is for the mature, who by constant use have trained themselves to distinguish good from evil. (Hebrews 5:13-14)

See it buried in his exasperation? He says solid food is for the mature.

Knowledge and Spiritual Maturity

You'll find as many different ideas on maturity as there are people. I know what my son David thinks: it's how much you know that makes you mature. No wonder he asks "Why?" David has decided that if he knows everything he'll achieve his ultimate goal: "Do it myself!"

The author of Hebrews did want his flock to know some things. He says that infants do not know the teachings of righteousness; mature people do. The things he calls "elementary" teaching in chapter 6 have been the study of many Ph.D. dissertations. The writer of Hebrews even wants his listeners to become teachers, but he knows that knowledge is only the first step of biblical maturity.

This is lost on many Christians. Many hold the belief that spiritual maturity is a function of biblical knowledge. When pushed, we intuitively understand this to be false. Take my friend Melissa's fifth-grade Sunday-school class. In order to win the prize for most Scripture memorized, an enterprising young fellow rattled off lists of genealogy from 1 Chronicles. When I asked what the teachers did, Melissa said, "Well, we had to give him the prize. He did what we asked."

I wonder if the same process doesn't continue in seminaries on a somewhat more sophisticated level. Students are given vast religious knowledge but a tiny understanding of why. This becomes a spiritual danger, for knowledge alone tends to makes us think we no longer need God.

Maturity and Age

David has another idea about maturity. For him maturity is age. That's why in our house we're still counting years in halves, as in "I'm four *and a half.*" When I missed a whole year, I'd deleted 25 percent of David's life, and by implication forgot the most significant holiday of the year—a birthday. No wonder he was upset. For David age is the attainment of respect, responsibility and getting to have a knife at the table like his big brother.

There is some truth to David's idea. His big brother can use a knife at the table because his dexterity ensures he'll not cut off his finger—a function of age. But David has confused age with maturity. Maturity is the ingredient that makes it less likely his big brother will use his knife as a sword at the table.

The same is true of spiritual maturity. Many think it's a function of age, how old you are or how long you have been a Christian. Certainly the Bible calls for the leaders of churches to be elders, not youngers, and this was in part a function of age. Elders are people who have been around, have seen some things, have dealt with some hard issues. Anyone with half a wit develops some maturity through the natural passages of life. But if age determined spiritual maturity we would have many more mature Christians.

Constant Use and Training

The book of Hebrews says it's through practice that maturity develops; the writer uses the words *constant use* and *training,* words I tend to think of as dreary.

If you're like me, you long for spiritual growth to be direct, easy and painless. It would even be nice to find brief detours into earthly success along life's way. I don't want to be on the road; I want to arrive. Like my children, I have an insatiable desire to know "when are we going to get there?" Never mind that I don't really know where *there* is.

I also want to be big, just like my kids do. I have the same sense they do that if I'm big my struggles will be over. But as any grownup knows, when you get big, you get bigger problems.

These twin desires—to arrive and to be spiritually big—pull me the way of the quick spiritual fix. I'm drawn to books with immediate answers, songs that thrill and weekend conferences that give "Seven Steps to Perfect Christianity." Those things make me feel as if I've gotten there without really doing the training.

Practicing our faith in the day to day is what makes us grow. Notice that the word *practicing* implies that we are going to make mistakes. We'll try things; some will work, others won't. The important thing—the successful thing—is to keep going. It's not flashy, but it's real.

Maturity and Sight

But practice alone is not spiritual maturity; it's only the preparation for spiritual maturity. One can blindly practice the teachings but not be spiritually mature. Just ask the Pharisees. They practiced and practiced, but only for practicing's sake. They thought it was to look good, not to know good. And when it came time to see, they couldn't. *How could they not see him?* I find myself thinking. They had prayed he would come. He walked with them. He ate in their homes, and yet it was the religious people—the ones who practiced their faith— who couldn't see. He stood before them; he healed broken bodies, broken hearts, broken lives, and they missed it, not because they ignored him, but because they thought him evil. The Pharisees did not know good from evil.

I'm not far from them. How often I've missed Jesus when he was trying to speak to me. It's as if I told him, "Lord, don't bother me now, I'm busy having a quiet time." The goal of practice and training is to see Jesus when he shows up, so we can see what's a door he's opened or what's just an open elevator shaft; so we see him in others and don't merely stare through them; so we know the difference between his voice and our thoughts. Ultimately this discernment, this spiritual sight, is true spiritual maturity.

Remember what the writer of Hebrews says: real spiritual

maturity is constant use of scriptural truth so that we can discern good from evil—spiritual sight. After he got this off his chest he quit his digression in the middle of chapter 6 and got back to explaining the priesthood of Jesus.

David, on the other hand, never did get back on track. He just left his noodles on his plate.